INSIGHTS FROM

THE PSALMS

III

by

Dr. John T. Willis

Published By
BIBLICAL RESEARCH PRESS
774 East North 15th Street
Abilene, Texas
79601

Insights From

THE PSALMS III

By John T. Willis

Copyright © 1974
Biblical Research Press

Library of Congress Catalog Card No. 73-93946

PREFACE

These three booklets on the PSALMS have been designed to aid the serious adult student of the Bible in growing in a knowledge of the word of God and in growing spiritually. The comments on each psalm should be studied in light of the biblical text itself. The author has used the RSV throughout.

Ninety-two of the 150 psalms have been treated at some length in these three volumes: 24 in Volume I, 35 in Volume II, and 33 in Volume III. It is felt that although not every psalm has been treated, the most representative psalms have, so that the student will have a fairly clear grasp of the nature of the psalms and the problems in them after studying these lessons. Of course, the avid Bible reader will want to study each and every psalm.

The three volumes here presented are the result of approximately fifteen years of careful study and teaching of this material. The writer looks forward to much deeper insights in the years to come. However, I do not feel this work could have come to completion without the patience and encouragement of the members of my family: My wife Evelyn, my children David, Debbie, Tim, and Paul, my mother-in-law Mrs. W. E. Forrest of Fort Worth, and my parents Mr. and Mrs. Cullen Willis of Cross Plains. To them I express my sincerest love and gratitude for any and every part they had in this venture. I am also grateful to my secretaries, Bonnie McQueen and Linda Nail, for typing the manuscripts.

John T. Willis

TABLE OF CONTENTS

Lesson I

THE MOURNFUL SEEK COMFORT IN GOD (I)

"For his anger is but for a moment,
and his favor is for a lifetime,
Weeping may tarry for the night,
but joy comes with the morning." (Psalm 30:5).

Men come before God with a great variety of feelings and needs. This variety is beautifully represented by the different ways in which the psalmists approach God. In Volume II, Lessons VIII-XIII, attention has been called to *sinners* who come to God confessing their iniquities and seeking forgiveness, the *joyful* who give God thanks, the *discouraged* who plead for God's help, and those that are persecuted who approach God asking him to bring vengeance on their adversaries. The first six lessons of the present volume deal with psalms in which other types of worshippers approach God. In the first two *lessons,* attention is focused on the mournful and weeping, who come to God seeking comfort and emotional relief.

Psalm 80

This psalm was composed by a group of worshippers (note the first person plural "we," "us," "our," etc., in vss. 2,3,6,7,18,19), who refer to themselves as "God's people" (v. 4). They had recently been overthrown by malicious enemies (vss. 6,12,16), who are compared with wild boars and beasts of the field (v. 13). Since the names that are used for God's people are "Israel," "Joseph" (v. 1), "Ephraim,"

"Benjamin," and "Manasseh" (v. 2), it is likely that the historical event lying behind this psalm was, the fall of Galilee and Gilead to Assyria in 732 B. C. (see *II Kings* 15:29) or the fall of Samaria to Assyria in 721 B. C. (see *II Kings* 17:1-6), and not the fall of Jerusalem to Babylon in 587 B. C. Israel had grievously sinned, and God had demonstrated his anger against his people by sending the enemy (vss. 4,18) to break down the walls of his vine (v. 12) and to burn it with fire (v. 16). The prayer that God "restore" his people (vss. 3,7,19) may indicate that those who composed this psalm had been carried into Assyrian captivity, or had fled to Judah to escape captivity and thus were no longer living in their native land.

There is a recurring refrain or chorus in vss. 3,7, and 19:

"Restore us, O God;
let thy face shine, that we may be saved!"

The appeal that God "let his face shine" (see *Psalm* 31:16) apparently is a prayer that he "be gracious to" his people and "bless" them. This seems to be confirmed by the synonymous parallelism in *Numbers* 6:24-25:

"The Lord bless you and keep you:
The Lord make his face to shine upon you,
and be gracious to you,"

and in *Psalm* 67:1:

"May God be gracious to us and bless us
and make his face to shine upon us."

The recurring refrain in *Psalm* 80 divides the song naturally into three parts. First, God's people pray that God will intervene to save and restore them (vss. 1-3). Here God is pictured as a shepherd, and Israel as his flock (v. 1). This figure is used frequently in the Old (*Genesis* 49:24; *Psalm* 77:20; *Isaiah* 40:11; 63:11) and New Testaments (*John* 10:1-18; *Luke* 15:3-7; *I Peter* 5:1-4). God is also depicted as a king, and Israel as his army (vss. 1-2). He is said to be "enthroned upon the cherubim." Among other things, the ark of the covenant was considered to be the Lord's throne-chariot (symbolically), and God was viewed as sitting enthroned above (or upon, or between) the cherubim above the ark (see *I Samuel* 4:4; *II Samuel* 6:2; and compare these with *Numbers* 7:89). As king, God led his army to victory against their enemies (see especially *I Samuel* 4:1-8; *Numbers* 10:35; 14:44; *II Samuel* 11:11; 15:24). In the ancient Near East, kings were frequently called shepherds, and this was also true in Israel (*II Samuel* 5:2; *Psalm* 78:71).

Second, the worshippers mourn grievously over their present misfortunes (vss. 4-7). They are convinced that their suffering is due to their many and heinous sins for which God is punishing them severely. But they insist that they have learned their lesson, repented, and sought the Lord's forgiveness. Yet, he keeps on refusing to answer their prayers for deliverance. So they cry, "*How long* wilt thou be angry with thy people's prayers?" (v. 4). They declare that the genuineness of their repentance is proved by the fact that their food and drink is continually tears (v. 5). And they bemoan the fact that, although they are God's people, their enemies constantly ridicule them (v. 6).

Third, they appeal to God to restore his "vine" (his people) to its former position and glory in the land of Canaan (vss. 8-19). The idea of God as the husbandman and his people as his vine is common in both Old (*Hosea* 9:16-10:1; *Isaiah* 3:14; 5:1-7; *Jeremiah* 2:21; 12:10; *Ezekiel* 17) and New Testaments (*John* 15:1-11). In our psalm, the singers review the history of God's dealing with his vine. (a) The vine did not originate in Canaan under God's care, but in Egypt. God took that vine (which was already in existence) and brought it out of Egypt at the exodus (v. 8). (b) God cleared the ground in Canaan for his vine by driving out the nations before his people, and then he transplanted his vine there. It grew into a huge and luxuriant plant that extended from the Mediterranean Sea to the Euphrates (vss. 8-11). Historically, this covers the period from Joshua and the conquest to David and Solomon, because Solomon's kingdom extended from the Mediterranean to the Euphrates (see *Genesis* 15:18; *Deuteronomy* 1:7; 11:24; *Joshua* 1:4; *I Kings* 4:21,24; *Psalm* 72:8), which is the extent of the territory covered by the vine in v. 11. (c) But now, the protective walls around the vine have been broken down (v. 12), enemies (v. 12) and wild beasts (v. 13) have eaten its fruit, and it has been burned with fire (v. 16). These figures apparently refer to a massive devastation of the land, so probably to the invasion of Tiglath-pileser III of Assyria in 732 B. C., or to the invasion of Shalmaneser V and Sargon II of Assyria in 724-721 B. C. (see above for the historical background).

The worshippers plead earnestly for God to intercede in their behalf. It is assumed that he lives in heaven and looks down on earth to see what is taking place (v. 14; see *Psalms* 14:2=53:2; 113:6). In their appeal to God for help, they use two word-plays. (a) They urge him to "turn again" to them (v. 14), and promise that they will never "turn back" from him again, as they had done when they lived in Canaan (v. 18). (b) They recall that he had planted his vine with his "right hand" (v. 15, evidently symbolizing God's special care in establishing Israel in Canaan), and now beg him to let his "hand" be upon the man of his "right hand" (v. 17). Some think that "the man (Hebrew *'ish*) of his right hand (Hebrew *yamin*)" is a word play on "Benjamin" (see v. 2), which is a compound of two Hebrew words, *ben* meaning "son," and *yamin* meaning "right hand." However, it is more likely that this expression was a stereotyped title for an Israelite or Judean king in Old Testament times. There is evidence for this in *Psalm* 110:1:

> "The Lord (i.e., God) says to my lord (i.e., the king):
>   'Sit at my right hand,
>   till I make your enemies your footstool'."

If the authors of this psalm are in Assyria where they have been carried captive, this king is probably Hoshea of Israel, but if they are in Judah where they have fled for refuge from the Assyrians, he is probably Hezekiah.

Psalm 137

The historical setting of *Psalm* 137 is similar to that lying behind *Psalm* 80, but not identical. *Psalm* 137 was composed by a group of worshippers (note the first person plural "we," "us," "our," etc., in vss. 1,2,3,4,8). The first person singular in vss. 5-6 probably does not represent an individual as author of the psalm, but rather the attitude of each and every individual in the group responsible for this song. These worshippers had recently been carried from Jerusalem (Zion, vss. 1,3,5,6,7) into Babylonian captivity (vss. 1,4,8). They vividly recall how the Edomites had joined the Babylonians in the siege of Jerusalem (see *Ezekiel* 25:12; 35:3-5; *Obadiah* 8-14; *Lamentations* 4:21-22) and had urged on the Babylonians, saying:

"Rase it, Rase it!
Down to its foundations!" (v. 7).

Now, while the Jews rest or live under the shade of willows somewhere in Babylon (v. 2), their Babylonian captors make fun of them because of their love for Jerusalem, and in jest force them to sing one of the songs of Zion (vss. 3-4). The Jews are helpless, and can only mourn their pitiable condition (v. 1). This song must have been composed shortly after the captivity of Jehoiachin and the 10,000 leading citizens of Jerusalem in 598 B. C. (see *II Kings* 24:10-17), or more likely shortly after the destruction of Jerusalem and the temple in 587 B. C. (see *II Kings* 25:1-21). The authors are temple singers (possibly priests, vss. 3-4), who accompanied their songs with the lyre (v. 2).

This psalm falls naturally into three parts containing three verses each. (1) They describe the miserable condition to which the Babylonians had subjected them (vss. 1-3). The terrible scenes connected with the fall of Jerusalem were still fresh on their minds and made them weep (v. 1). They were separated from the temple, and therefore could not sing the "songs of Zion," which were intended for temple worship. Therefore, they hung up their lyres (v. 2). But, to torment them, their Babylonian captors forced them to sing the songs of Zion in jest (v. 3), which is equivalent to saying in ridicule and mockery, "Where is your God?" On the basis of the word "there" in vss. 1,2,3 (referring to Babylon), some scholars think this psalm was not written until the authors had left Babylon. But v. 4 indicates that they had not returned to Jerusalem, for they are still in a "foreign land."

Perhaps "there" refers to one of the "waters" (irrigation canals) of Babylon where this band of captives was allowed to rest on its way from Jerusalem to their final dwelling place in Babylon.

(2) The Jewish captives vow unswerving allegiance to Jerusalem as long as they live (vss. 4-6). Apparently, they regard Babylon as an unclean land (just as Amos regarded Assyria as unclean, see *Amos* 7:17), and thus refuse to sing one of the songs of Zion there (v. 4). Individually, they subject themselves voluntarily and gladly to a self-curse. If they do not hold Jerusalem in the highest esteem continually, they pray that their right hand might wither and their tongue cleave to the roof of their mouth (vss. 5-6). This was the strongest self-imprecation that these temple singers could take, because they played their lyres with their right hands and sang the songs of Zion with their tongues. (Note the inverted parallelism in vss. 5-6b).

(3) The devastated captives pray that God will destroy Edom and Babylon for the malicious way in which they had overthrown Jerusalem (vss. 7-9). They had vowed to "remember" Jerusalem (v. 6), and now they pray that the Lord would "remember" how the Edomites had urged the Babylonians on as they destroyed Jerusalem (v. 7). They affirm that the nation that renders to Babylon what she had rendered to Jerusalem would be blessed (v. 8). The gleeful anticipation of having Babylonian children dashed against a rock (v. 9) raises problems for the Christian reader. However, the following considerations need to be kept in mind. (a) Those who sing this song had probably recently watched helplessly as some of their own children had been dashed to death against rocks by the Babylonians. (b) It was a common practice in ancient warfare to kill children of the enemy by dashing them against rocks (*II Kings* 8:12; *Hosea* 10:14), and it may be that the authors of this psalm simply used familiar language to convey their wish that their destroyers might be destroyed, and that their captors might become captives. (c) If the thoughts expressed in *Psalm* 137:7-9 represent the ideas of angry Jews rather that inspired ideas from God, then *Psalm* 137 was not *originally composed* under inspiration,

but rather was included in the Old Testament canon under divine guidance or inspiration. If this is the case, then every psalm should be scrutinized on the basis of pre-established valid criteria to determine which were *originally* inspired and which were included by inspiration. This is important in a practical way, because a person needs to be able to determine which biblical texts can serve as guides for his life, and which are to be used only as illustrations of sinful attitudes, emotions, or actions which he must avoid (as e.g., David's sins against Bathsheba and Uriah, II Samuel 11). (d) Further suggestions on ways of looking at this problem are made at the end of Lesson XIII in Volume II, and the reader is urged to study these carefully before reaching a decision on this matter.

REVIEW QUESTIONS

1. Discuss the historical background of *Psalm* 80. What events in Israel's history could be assumed here? Which do you think is the most likely? Give your reasons.

2. What is the meaning of the expression, "let thy (i.e., God's) face shine," in *Psalm* 80:3,7,19? Give good reasons for your conclusion. See *Psalms* 31:16; 67:1; *Numbers* 6:24-25.

3. Give a three point outline of *Psalm* 80, then tell in your own words the content of this psalm.

4. What three figures are used in *Psalm* 80 to depict the relationship between God and his people? Discuss the significance of each of these in detail, and state their relevance to New Testament thought.

5. Discuss the meaning of the phrase, "Thou (i.e., God) who art enthroned upon the cherubim," in *Psalm* 80:1. See also *I Samuel* 4:4; *II Samuel* 6:2.

6. Outline the history of Israel pictured under the figure of the vine in *Psalm* 80:8-16. Why is this significant for the thought the authors of this psalm are trying to convey?

7. Who is "the man of thy (i.e., God's) right hand" in *Psalm* 80:17? See *Psalm* 110:1. Do your own research and find other ideas as to the meaning of this phrase.

8. Discuss the historical background of *Psalm* 137. Give as many details as the text of this psalm allows.

9. Give a three point outline of *Psalm* 137, and tell in your own words the content of this psalm.

10. To what does the word "there" in *Psalm* 137:1, 2, 3 refer? Discuss various views on this, and show how this is connected with determining the date and historical setting of this psalm.

11. Discuss the curses uttered against Edom and Babylon in *Psalm* 137:7-9. How do you think a Christian is to view these? Can such a psalm as this be inspired by God? Discuss in detail. See Volume II, Lesson XIII.

Lesson II

THE MOURNFUL SEEK COMFORT IN
GOD (II)

"Blessed are those who mourn, for they shall be comforted."
(Matthew 5:4).

Psalm 30

The heading of this psalm suggests that it was composed for or sung at the dedication of the temple. This would place its origin no earlier than 165 B. C., when Judas Maccabaeus purified and dedicated the temple, after it had been desecrated by the Seleucid king, Antiochus IV Epiphanes, in 168 B. C. (see *I Maccabees* 4:35-59; *John* 10:22 presupposes this event). However, the content of the psalm hardly warrants this historical setting.

Psalm 30 was composed by an individual who had been stricken by a serious illness, which had brought him very close to death (vss. 2, 3, 9). This was the means God used to punish him (vss. 5, 7) for his pride (v. 6), and when he was stricken, his enemies rejoiced over his calamity (v. 1). As he suffered from his disease, from the Lord's anger and withdrawal, and from his enemies' taunts, the poet wept and mourned bitterly (vss. 5, 11), and urged God to deliver him from his afflictions (vss. 2, 8-10) in order that he might praise him (v. 9). The Lord answered his prayers and saved him from death (vss. 2-3, 11). Out of his experience, the author learned the marvelous lesson that God's anger is merely a secondary and passing aspect of his nature, and that the primary feature of his character is grace (v. 10) and loving favor (v. 5). This is emphasized by the statements made at the end of each division of the song:

> "For his anger is but for a moment,
>   and his favor is for a lifetime.
> Weeping may tarry for the night,
>   but joy comes with the morning." (v. 5).
> "Thou hast turned for me my mourning into dancing;
>   thou hast loosed my sackcloth
>   and girded me with gladness." (v. 11).

In light of this, the psalmist praises God openly (v. 12), and urges his fellow worshippers to do likewise (v. 4).

Psalm 30, then, falls naturally into two parts: vss. 1-5 and 6-12. Each division begins with a description of the poet's pitiable condition, and ends with praise to God for delivering him. In vss. 1-5, the author gives a brief general description of his desperate situation. He had been brought to the very edge of Sheol or the Pit (v. 3), i.e., death, because of God's anger (v. 5), and his enemies were rejoicing over him (v. 1). But he cried to the Lord, and the Lord healed him (v. 2), drew him up (v. 1) or brought him up from Sheol (v. 3), and restored him to life (v. 3). He concludes from this that God's anger is transient, but his favor or grace is permanent (v. 5), and thus he summons his fellow saints to praise God for what he had done for him (v. 4).

In vss. 6-12, the psalmist describes his experience in greater detail. He had been very prosperous, and this had led him to assume that he would never be moved and that God had firmly established him (vss. 6-7a), in other words, he had become proud and self-satisfied. But suddenly, God hid his face from him, i.e., he withdrew his protection from him and smote him with severe disease for his pride (v. 7b). Then the poet cried out for the Lord's grace and help (v. 10). To persuade God not to let him die, he asks him what can be gained by his death. In the grave, he could not praise God and tell others of his mighty works; thus it would seem logical to restore him to health (v. 9). The Lord heard his pleas and delivered him, and now the psalmist resolves to give God thanks "for ever" (vss. 11-12). Synonymous parallelism shows that the word "soul" in vss. 3 and 12 means "the whole person," and not the inner, eternal part of man. "For ever" in v. 12 can hardly mean endless time, since the psalmist died long ago. The context indicates that it refers to the rest of his life (see *I Samuel* 1:11, 22, 28).

Psalm 6

The setting and thought of this psalm are very similar to that found in *Psalm* 30. The poet is very sick and feels that he will soon die (vss. 2, 4-5). His illness is God's means of punishing him for his sin (v. 1). His enemies rejoice over his misfortune (vss. 7, 8, 10). Thus, the author's problems are complex and heavy to bear. He constantly weeps and mourns over his pitiable condition. He cries out:

> "I am weary with my moaning;
>   every night I flood my bed with tears;
> I drench my couch with my weeping.
> My eye wastes away because of grief,
>   it grows weak because of all my foes."
>   (vss. 6-7; see also v. 8).

But then something happens, and the psalmist is certain that God has heard his prayer and that his enemies will be put to shame for rejoicing over his calamity (vss. 8-10).

Psalm 6 falls naturally into two divisions: (1) the poet describes his miserable situation, and pleads with God to deliver him (vss. 1-7); (2) he praises God for answering his prayer, and expresses his assurance that his enemies will be put to shame (vss. 8-10).

In vss. 1-7, the poet begs God to quit dealing with him on the basis of anger and wrath (v. 1), and to deal with him on the basis of grace (v. 2) and steadfast love (v. 4). He gives three reasons to persuade God to do this. (a) He is miserable in his present condition. He is languishing (v. 2), his bones and his soul are troubled (vss. 2, 3), and he is weary and weak from ceaseless weeping and moaning (vss. 6, 7). The word "soul" in v. 3 means the whole person. (b) Primarily and fundamentally, God is not a God of anger, but of steadfast love (v. 4). "For the sake of" his steadfast love, the author prays for deliverance. (c) In the grave, it is impossible for one to praise God to his fellowmen on earth. Since the psalmist is one who praises God, he begs him to spare his life (v. 5).

In light of the poet's desperate cries for help in vss. 1-7, his certainty that God had heard his prayer in vss. 8-10 is somewhat difficult to explain. (1) Some scholars argue that God had not really answered his prayer when he spoke the words recorded in vss. 8-10, but he was so sure he would that he stated them as if God had already answered him. (2) Others think that a cult prophet or a priest delivered an oracle between vss. 7 and 8, stating that God had answered the psalmist's prayer, and thus vss. 8-10 contain the poet's response to that oracle. Whatever the correct explanation may be, it should be noted that although God has answered the psalmist's prayer, his enemies still threaten him, and thus he looks forward to their withdrawal from him and to their overthrow through God's power (vss. 8, 10).

Psalm 22

Since the setting and concepts of *Psalm* 22 are so similar to those found in *Psalms* 30 and 6, the comments made above will prove very helpful in analyzing this song. The psalmist is oppressed by three problems. (1) He is very sick, probably with a high fever, and feels that he is near death (vss. 14-17). (2) He feels that God has deserted him, because no matter how much he begs God to help him, there is no reply (vss. 1-2, 11, 15, 19). (3) His enemies have unleashed a malicious attack against him. They despise and mock him because he claims that he trusts in God, but God does not help him (vss. 6-8). As he hangs between life and death, they surround him, gloat over his miserable condition, and eagerly await his death (vss. 12-13, 16-18, 20-21). It is worthy of note that these are the very same problems that faced the authors of *Psalms* 30 and 6.

Also like *Psalms* 30 and 6, *Psalm* 22 naturally falls into two parts. (1) The author describes his afflictions, and begs God to deliver him (vss. 1-21). (2) He praises God before his fellow worshippers for answering his prayer, and declares that this deliverance will be a means of converting the nations to the worship of the true God (vss. 22-31).

In vss. 1-21, the poet is struck by the seeming inconsistency of God's actions. He cries out to God day and night to give him rest from his disease, but there is no response (vss. 1-2). And *yet* (v. 3), when Israelites called on God in former generations, he saved them and did not disappoint them as he is now disappointing the psalmist (vss. 3-5). When God delivered his worshippers, they always praised him, as this sufferer is willing to do. Thus, the invisible Lord, who was regarded as "enthroned" upon the cherubim of the ark (*I Samuel* 4:4; *II Samuel* 6:2; *Psalm* 99:1), can be said to have been "enthroned on the praises of Israel" throughout the centuries (v. 3). And the psalmist wishes to add his praises to those of the multitudes that have gone before, when the Lord intervenes and delivers him.

As things now stand, the poet feels stripped of his humanity: "I am a worm, and no man" (v. 6). His enemies scorn him and despise him (v. 6). They mock at him, make faces at him, and wag their heads at him (v. 7). They laugh at him because he has committed his cause to the Lord, and yet the Lord has made no reply (v. 8). And *yet* (v. 9), God had been his protector from the very moment he was born, and he had been God's servant ever since he could remember. It just does not make sense for God to abandon him now! (vss. 9-11).

The present circumstances are as bad as they can be, short of death itself. The poet's enemies have surrounded him and are ready for the kill. In graphic animal imagery, he compares them with many strong bulls of Bashan or wild oxen (vss. 12, 21), ravening and roaring lions (vss. 13, 21), and hungry dogs (vss. 16, 20). His illness has reached the critical state. He is racked with fever (vss. 14-15), he has lost all his vitality (v. 15), and he has lost so much weight that one can count his bones as they stick out from his body (v. 17). God himself has laid him "in the dust of death" (v. 15), and his enemies are so certain he will die that they cast lots to see who will receive the various garments that he is about to leave behind (v. 18). With no one else to help, and wholly unable to help himself, the psalmist turns to the Lord in a final desperate effort to save his life (vss. 11, 19).

In vss. 22-31, the author praises God because he has heard his prayer and has delivered him from death and all his afflictions. The content and the entire tone of this section are so different from vss. 1-21 that several scholars have argued that originally vss. 1-21 and 22-31 were two independent psalms, which later have been combined. However, *Psalm* 6 (and other psalms also) indicates that this type of structure is common in such psalms. Therefore, we are thrown back on the same two explanations suggested in connection with *Psalm* 6. Some scholars think that when the author of *Psalm* 22:22-31 uttered the words found there, he had not yet actually experienced God's deliverance, but had become so sure that God would save him that he expressed his hopes in the past tense (Hebrew perfect) as if they had already happened. However, in light of the vividness of vss. 22-31, it seems more likely that a cult prophet of priest delivered an oracle between vss. 21 and 22, declaring that God had answered the psalmist's pleas, and then vss. 22-31 contain the poet's response to this oracle.

For the psalmist, three good things naturally flow from God's having delivered him from death. (1) He will tell his fellow worshippers, especially those who are suffering similar afflictions, what God had done for him (vss. 22, 25). (2) He will encourage those who are afflicted to join him in praising God for being the deliverer of the afflicted (vss. 23-24, 26). (3) All the earth will learn from this object lesson that Israel's God is the God of the whole world, and they will join Israel in worshipping him (vss. 27-28). In fact, God's powerful deliverance of this man who faced insuperable obstacles is so magnificent that it will be told over and over again to "the coming generation," to "a people yet unborn" (vss. 30-31). Some scholars have taken the statements in v. 29 to mean that even in Sheol ("the dust," i.e., the grave) the dead will praise God. If this is the case, then it would differ from the thought expressed in *Psalm* 6:5:

"For in death there is no remembrance of thee;
in Sheol who can give thee praise?"

However, it is more likely that v. 29 means that men destined to die (i.e., "mortal men") will praise God for what he has done for the psalmist.

Three terms used in this psalm deserve brief attention. (1) The word "heart" appears in vss. 14 and 26. In both passages, it is quite clear that it refers to the whole person. To say *"my heart* is like wax" is virtually the same as to say *"I* am poured out like water" (v. 14). And "may your *hearts* live for ever" means "may *you* live for ever" (v. 26). (2) The word "soul" is used in vss. 20-21. Synonymous parallelism shows that it is equivalent to "my life" in v. 20, and to "me" in v. 21. So, like "heart," the word "soul" means the whole person, and not the inner spiritual part of man. (3) In v. 26, the psalmist says to his fellow worshippers, "May your hearts live *for ever!*" Yet, those worshippers died long ago, and the psalmist knew they would die when he uttered these words! Thus, "for ever" here does not mean "endless life," but a long life.

A careful study of *Psalm* 22 shows that it is not a prediction of the coming of Christ, but rather the utterances of a man undergoing severe affliction (vss. 1-21), and this man's exuberant joy upon being delivered (vss. 22-31). And yet, several verses in this psalm are used by Christ or applied to Christ in the New Testament. (1) Christ quotes v. 1 while hanging on the cross (*Matthew* 27:46; *Mark* 15:34). (2) The gospel writers state that the Roman soldiers mocked Jesus (*Mark* 15:20), and that those who passed by as he hung on the cross wagged their heads at him and derided him (*Matthew* 27:39; *Mark* 15:29). Our psalmist says similar things about the the way his enemies treated him in v. 7; however, the New Testament nowhere quotes v. 7 and applies it to Christ. (3) As Jesus hung on the cross, the chief priests, scribes, and elders of the Jews cried out, "He trusts in God; let God deliver him now, if he desires him" (*Matthew* 27:43; see also *Luke* 23:35). Our poet relates similar words that were spoken against him by his enemies in v. 8; and yet again, the New Testament does not quote v. 8 and apply it to

Christ. (4) Some scholars think that v. 15 is the basis for the statement made in *John* 19:28: "After this Jesus, knowing that all was finished, said (to fulfil the scripture), 'I thirst'." If this is the case, the quotation "I thirst" certainly is not taken directly from *Psalm* 22:15 (or for that matter from any other Old Testament text). But it is also quite likely that John had *Psalm* 69:21 in mind, as the reference to "vinegar" in *John* 10:29 would suggest. (5) As Jesus hung on the cross, the Roman soldiers cast lots to see who would receive his garments (*Matthew* 26:35; *Mark* 15:24; *Luke* 23:34). John says that "this was to fulfil the scripture,

> 'They parted my garments among them,
> and for my clothing they cast lots'." (*John* 19:24).

This is a quotation from *Psalm* 22:18. (6) The author of the book of Hebrews quotes *Psalm* 22:22 in *Hebrews* 2:12:

> "I will proclaim thy name to my brethren,
> in the midst of the congregation I will praise thee."

In its Old Testament context, the psalmist here resolves to tell his fellow worshippers how God had delivered him from terrible calamity. But the author of the book of Hebrews uses the word "I" to apply to Christ, and the word "brethren" to refer to Christians, in order to convey the idea that Christ "is not ashamed to call them (i.e., Christians) brethren." (It might be mentioned in passing that some scholars find an allusion to *Psalm* 22:16 in texts like *Luke* 23:33 and *John* 20:27. However, the text of *Psalm* 22:16 is problematic at this point, and there can be no certainty as to whether New Testament writers actually alluded to this verse).

For a detailed study of the various ways that the New Testament uses the Old, the reader is invited to read the booklet entitled *My Servants, the Prophets*, Volume II, Lessons VII and VIII, by the present author. In view of the suggestions made there, the following observations may be made on the use of *Psalm* 22 in the New Testament. (a) Jesus and the gospel writers saw several striking *parallels* between the severe suffering of the author of *Psalm* 22 and Christ's suffering on the cross, and therefore they intentionally used the language of *Psalm* 22 in describing Christ's sufferings on the cross. (2) There are probably two reasons why they chose this Old Testament terminology. First, it was already familiar to their hearers. Second, the customary ways of treating one's foes in the days of the psalmist and in the days of Jesus were identical or very similar. For example, it was customary to mock or deride one's enemy, and to emphasize that his trust in God was futile, in order to break down his morale. It was customary for those who yearned for and expected their enemy to die to cast lots for his clothing to see who would get each piece. (3) There are different ways in which an Old Testament text can be *fulfilled* in the New. It may be fulfilled *literally*. But it may also be fulfilled *typologically,* and this seems to be the case with *Psalm* 22:18 in *John* 19:24. (4) *Hebrews* 2:12 is thinking of different people (Christ and Christians) from those originally meant in *Psalm* 22:22 (the psalmist and his fellow worshippers). Thus, here the New Testament writer is more concerned with the "words" of the Old Testament text he is quoting than with the "original meaning."

REVIEW QUESTIONS

1. What three problems were confronted by the authors of *Psalms* 30, 6, and 22? Have you ever had to face similar problems? Share your experiences with the class.

2. Study *Psalm* 30:5, 11 very carefully. What important lesson do these verses teach concerning God's primary character? Discuss. Do your preacher or elders or Bible class teachers continually emphasize this fundamental aspect of God's character in their preaching and teaching?

3. Give a two point outline of *Psalm* 30, and tell in your own words the content of this psalm.

4. Give a two point outline of *Psalm* 6, and tell in your own words the content of this psalm. How do you reconcile the poet's pleas in the first part of the psalm with his thanksgiving for deliverance in the last?

5. What three reasons does the author of *Psalm* 6 give to induce God to deliver him from his afflictions? Discuss the validity of Christians trying to persuade God to answer their prayers by using this kind of reasoning.

6. What two inconsistencies in God's actions does the author of *Psalm* 22 describe? See vss. 1-5 and 6-11. Discuss the significance of this in his prayer.

7. With what three animals does the author of *Psalm* 22 compare his enemies? See verses 12-13, 16-21. Use a concordance and see if this kind of imagery is used elsewhere in the Psalms, in the Old Testament, and in the New Testament. Share at least one passage in each of these portions of scripture with the class.

8. After God delivers the psalmist who wrote *Psalm* 22, what three things does the psalmist expect to naturally result from this deliverance? See vss. 22-31. Can Christians do the same thing when God delivers them and blesses their lives? Discuss.

9. Discuss the meaning of the following words in *Psalm* 22: "heart" in vss. 14 and 26; "soul" in vss. 20-21; and "for ever" in v. 26. Use several commentaries, Bible encyclopedias, and books or journal articles in your research on this point.

10. List the six verses in *Psalm* 22 that in some way are alluded to in the New Testament, and give at least one verse in the New Testament where each is mentioned. Discuss the problem of *how* the New Testament uses each verse.

Lesson III

THE LONELY YEARN FOR GOD'S FRIENDSHIP

"I did not sit in the company of merrymakers,
nor did I rejoice;
I sat alone, because thy hand was upon me,
for thou hadst filled me with indignation." (Jeremiah
15:17).

Although there are multitudes of people on earth, circumstances can arise in which an individual feels completely isolated from God and man, even from his dearest friends and loved ones. Job experienced such feelings and said:

"He (i.e., God) has put my brethren far from me,
and my acquaintances are wholly estranged from me.
My kinsfolk and my close friends have failed me . . .
I am repulsive to my wife,
loathsome to the sons of my mother . . .
All my intimate friends abhor me,
and those whom I loved have turned against me."
(*Job* 19:13-14, 17, 19).

Likewise, Jeremiah cried:

"I hear many whispering.
Terror is on every side!
'Denounce him! Let us denounce him!'
say all my familiar friends,
watching for my fall." (*Jeremiah* 20:10).

Several psalmists underwent similar experiences, and in their utter loneliness strove for God's help and friendship. This lesson deals with two psalms, whose authors bore the heavy weight of a feeling of loneliness.

Psalm 31

Some scholars believe this psalm was originally two independent psalms: vss. 1-8 and 9-24, because vss. 5b-8 seem to suggest that God answered the poet's pleas in vss. 1-5a. If so, it would not make sense for him to resume his pleas in vss. 9ff. But there are two other explanations of this phenomenon. First, it is possible that the psalmist covers the same ground twice for the sake of emphasis. In that case, vss. 9-18 would be an expansion of vss. 1-5a, and vss. 19-24 an expansion of vss. 5b-8, and the psalm would take on an *abab* structure. Or second, it may be that vss. 5b, 7b-8 describe an earlier experience of the psalmist, and that vss. 1-5a, 6-7a, 9-24 describe his present experience. This last explanation seems to be the best, and is adopted in the present study.

The psalmist is burdened with many heavy problems. He is very sick (vss. 9-10). He is convinced that this is God's punishment for a terrible sin he has committed, and thus he is far away from God's presence (vss. 10, 22; it seems best to read "iniquity" in v. 10 following the original Hebrew, rather than "misery," which the RSV adopts, following the Greek Septuagint and the Syriac Peshitta). His enemies plot against him and yearn for his death (vss. 4, 11, 13, 15, 17-18, 20, 21, 23). But on top of all this, his neighbors and acquaintances avoid him, apparently because they too are convinced that his afflictions are God's punishment for his sin (v. 11).

Psalm 31 falls naturally into three parts. (1) The poet confidently places his trust in God to deliver him from his afflictions, as he had done on a former occasion (or on former occasions) (vss. 1-8). (2) He vividly describes his afflictions, and reaffirms his confidence that God will deliver him (vss. 9-18). (3) He praises God for having answered his prayer and for having delivered him out of all his troubles, and calls on his fellow worshippers to put their trust in God to deliver them out of all their calamities (vss. 19-24).

As has already been suggested, vss. 1-8 are hard to understand. Vss. 1-3 may be a frequently used prayer which this poet has adopted for the beginning of his song, because it appears almost verbatim in *Psalm* 71:1-3, and many thoughts expressed here are found in *Psalm* 18:1-2. the psalmist's fundamental prayer is that God will deliver him from his afflictions (vss. 1, 2, 4), and he offers three reasons why God should answer him. (a) The author's enemies are idol worshippers (v. 6) and have used clandestine means to overthrow him (vs. 4). Like hunters who have laid a net for their prey, his enemies have devised evil against him which will strike suddenly and without warning. (b) God delivered him on a former occasion, when he had been confronted with similar problems (vss. 5, 7-8). His enemies had made him feel cramped, as though he were in close quarters, but God had set him in a broad place (v. 8; see *Psalm* 18:19). (c) He commits himself wholly into God's care and trusts completely in him to deliver him (vss. 1, 2, 3, 4, 5, 6, 7).

The terminology used in this paragraph (and throughout the psalm) to describe God's character and God's relationship to the poet is.very instructive. The poet throws himself on God's righteousness (v. 1), faithfulness (v. 5), grace (v. 9), goodness (v. 19), and in particular his steadfast love (vss. 7, 16, 21). All of these terms convey virtually the same idea, viz., that the psalmist is not appealing to God to save him from his afflictions because of his own goodness, but "for his name's sake" (v. 3), i.e., in keeping with his character of love and mercy. The author refers to God as his "rock" (vss, 2, 3), "fortress" (vss. 2, 3), and "refuge" (vss. 1-2, 4, 19). All these terms suggest the thought that God is the worshipper's protector. "Rock" is a familiar name for God throughout the Old Testament (*Deuteronomy* 32:4, 15, 18, 30-31, 37; *I Samuel* 2:2; *Psalm* 18:2, 31, 46; etc.).

In vss. 9-19, the poet gives a detailed description of his troubles. He has been very sick for a long time (vss. 9-10). He is convinced that this is God's way of punishing him for his sins, and he concludes: "I am driven far from thy sight" (vss. 10, 22). His neighbors and best friends concur in this conclusion, and thus avoid the psalmist (v. 11), making him feel like a "broken vessel" which at one time was useful for carrying water or wine or grain, but now is of no use to anyone (v. 12). His enemies plot secretly against him (v. 13), proudly slander his good name before the people of the land (vss. 18, 20, 23), and seek to put him to shame (vss. 1, 17). But in spite of all these obstacles, the author reaffirms his steadfast trust in God to deliver him from his foes (vss. 14-17a), and to overthrow his enemies (vss. 17b-18). His plea, "Let thy face shine on thy servant" (v. 16), is a cry for God to be gracious to him and bless him, as is indicated by the synonymous parallelism in *Numbers* 6:24-25 and *Psalm* 67:1 (see also *Psalm* 80:3, 7, 19; the plea for God to be gracious in *Psalm* 31:9; and the parallelism in v. 16 with "save me"). This psalmist's expressions of trust are some of the most powerful to be found anywhere in scripture.:

> "My times are in thy hand" (v. 15).
> "Into thy hand I commit my spirit" (v. 5).

The last words that Jesus spoke on the cross recorded in scripture are these words found in v. 5 (*Luke* 23:46). It was natural for him to see a striking parallel between the complex afflictions that the psalmist had faced and his own sufferings on the cross.

Vss. 19-24 contain a song of thanksgiving by one who has already been delivered from his calamities. How can this be explained in light of the pleas for help in vss. 1-18? Some scholars think that the psalmist had not yet actually been delivered when he spoke these words, but was so sure that God would save him that he talked as if he had already done so. It seems more likely, however, that a priest or a cult prophet gave the poet a divine oracle between vss. 18 and 19, telling him that God had delivered him from his afflictions, and that vss. 19-24 are his response to that oracle.

In this song, first the psalmist praises God for working in his behalf because of his abundant goodness, and for protecting him from the secret plots and slanderous words of his enemies (vss. 19-20). In Old Testament thought, God has a "storehouse" or "treasure" or "treasury" for each of his blessings, like light, darkness, snow, hail, and the east wind

(*Job* 38:19, 22, 24). Here, the psalmist affirms that God has a storehouse where he "lays up" his goodness, to be brought forth when those who fear him need it (v. 19). The figures for God's protection of the author in v. 20 are graphic indeed: The Lord's protection is like a "covert" (i.e., a thick clump of bushes) and a "shelter" (i.e., an enclosed hut), which shielded the traveller from the sharp driving sand of a desert storm. Second, having learned from his own experience how God delivers one who trusts in him, the psalmist calls on his fellows to love God, be strong, and take courage in him, and warns them not to be proud as his enemies had been (vss. 23-24). He is keenly aware that God's deliverance of him was not done in private, and therefore that it would have a great effect on those who saw it or who would learn of it (v. 19).

Psalm 88

The author of this psalm is oppressed by many great burdens. He is suffering from a severe illness that has plagued him from childhood (v. 15), and now has brought him to the very threshold of death (vss. 3-6, 10-12, 15-17). He knows that it is a manifestation of the wrath of God upon him (vss. 6-7, 14, 16). All his friends and relatives have forsaken him, either because they are also convinced that his sickness proves the depth of his sin, or because it is so repulsive that they cannot stand to be around him (vss. 8, 18). Lonely and dejected, the full weight of his problems come crashing in upon him, and he weeps bitterly (vss. 3, 9, 15) and cries out to the Lord for help (vss. 1-2, 9, 13-14).

These cries for help apparently stand at the beginning of each of the three divisions of *Psalm* 88. In each division (vss. 1-9a, 9b-12, and 13-18), the psalmist describes his pitiable situation, and tries to induce God to intervene in his behalf. It is worthy of note that the poet never voices his confidence that God will hear his cry, and yet the very fact that he prays to him in his grief indicates that he must have believed that he would.

In vss. 1-9a, the author states that he continually pleads with God to hear him ("by day . . . in the night," v. 1). Then he gives several reasons why he thinks the Lord should deliver him. (1) His life is filled with troubles (v. 3). (2) He stands right on the threshold of death (vss. 3-6). (3) He is unable to help himself (v. 4—"I am a man who has no strength"; note also v. 8—"I am shut in so that I cannot escape"; and v. 15—"I am helpless"). (4) He has been afflicted, not merely with one powerful calamity, but with calamity after calamity, like great waves of the sea dashing upon the land (v. 7; see also vss. 16-17). Here, one is reminded of the series of troubles that came upon Job one after another (*Job* 1:13-19). (5) It is God himself who has brought these calamities upon him (v. 7), and who has caused his friends to shun him, so that he is alone and lonely (v. 8; see also v. 18).

In vss. 9b-12, the psalmist again declares that he never ceases to pray to God to help him ("every day," v. 9b). And here he gives another reason why God should deliver him from death and restore him to good health. The dead ("the shades") do not praise God, declare his steadfast love and faithfulness, or make known his wonders and saving help to men on earth (vss. 10-12, the argument is the same as that made in *Psalm* 6:4-5). Since the poet desires to praise God before others for his wonderful works in his behalf, he urges the Lord to deliver him from all his troubles that he might have a personal experience to relate.

In vss. 13-18, again the psalmist affirms that he begs God for help regularly ("in the morning," v. 13). And here he adds a final reason for God to deliver him. There is nothing good that can come from God's continual rejection and persecution of the author. So he asks:

"O Lord, why dost thou cast me off?
Why dost thou hide thy face from me?" (v. 14).

Psalm 88 is important because it contains a great deal of information concerning the Old Testament concept of the realm of the dead. The psalmist uses several terms to describe it, such as Sheol (v. 3), the Pit (vss. 4, 6), the grave (vss. 5, 11), the regions dark and deep (v. 6), Abaddon (v. 11), the darkness (v. 12), and the land of forgetfulness (v. 12). The real meaning of most of these terms is debated among scholars. Abaddon means "(place of) destruction," but it is not clear whether this means the place where those who destroyed (killed? died?) on earth descend, or the place where destruction of the dead takes place. The "land of forgetfulness" is also ambiguous. Does this mean that in time the living on earth forget the dead, or does it mean that the dead forget what God has done?

Our poet also makes some statements about what takes place in the realm of the dead which are quite interesting. (1) God does not remember the dead any more; they are cut off from his hand (v. 5). (2) God does not work wonders for the dead as he does for the living, and consequently "the shades" do not rise up to praise him like the living do (v. 10). (3) The dead do not declare the Lord's steadfast love and faithfulness, or make known his wonders and saving help (vss. 11-12). Or these verses could mean that the living cannot proclaim God's steadfast love, etc., to those in the grave; or that the dead cannot declare God's steadfast love and faithfulness (v. 11), because God's wonders and saving help are not known in the realm of the dead (v. 12).

In light of the context of *Psalm* 88, it would be a mistake to use this text dogmatically to shed light on the Old Testament concept of life after death, because the psalmist's main concern is to remind God of the difference between the appreciation for his words by a living man on earth and a man in the realm of the dead. He does not even broach the question of a judgment or of eternal life or eternal punishment.

REVIEW QUESTIONS

1. Discuss the problem of human loneliness in a world filled with people. Study carefully *Job* 19:13-14, 17, 19; and *Jeremiah* 20:10 on this problem. Have you ever experienced deep loneliness? Share your experience with the class.

2. List the burdens that the author of *Psalm* 31 was having to bear. Have you ever faced similar troubles? Share your present problems with the class, and get reactions from different people in the class.

3. Give a three point outline of *Psalm* 31, then tell in your own words the content of this psalm.

4. What three reasons does the author of *Psalm* 31:1-8 give God to induce him to answer his prayer? Should the Christian try to persuade God to answer him with similar arguments? Discuss at length.

5. What terms does the author of *Psalm* 31 use to describe God's character, and to denote God's relationship to him? What practical lessons do you receive from this to help you understand your own relationship to God?

6. In what two ways does the poet react to God's deliverance in *Psalm* 31:19-24? Do you feel that our reactions should be similar today? Discuss the practical implications of this for Christian living.

7. List the burdens borne by the author of *Psalm* 88. Are you presently burdened by similar afflictions? Share your problems with the class, openly seeking help and comfort from your fellow Christians. Are you afraid or ashamed to share your burdens with you brethren? How does *Psalm* 88 help you with this problem? Discuss at length.

8. Give a three point outline of *Psalm* 88, and then tell in your own words the content of this psalm.

9: List the seven reasons given by the author of *Psalm* 88 to persuade God to answer his prayer. Is it right for a Christian to use such inducements to persuade the Lord to answer his prayers? Discuss.

10. Discuss the concept of the realm of the dead as depicted in *Psalm* 88. Use several commentaries, and try to determine the meaning of each expression and of each statement. Do you feel this psalm is helpful in determining the Old Testament idea of life after death? Why? Give solid arguments for your position.

Lesson IV

GOD'S MENACED PEOPLE DESIRE RELIEF FROM THEIR FOES

"O Lord, how many are my foes!
Many are rising against me;
Many are saying of me,
'There is no help for him in God'." (Psalm 3:1-2).

The history of Israel, the church, and all mankind has been marred by wars and rumors of wars. Throughout Israel's life in the land of Canaan, she was frequently attacked by the nations around her, some large and some small. We have already studied *Psalms* 2 and 48, which come from such a time. In these psalms, the king and Zion respectively were the points of focus. Attention is now drawn to certain psalms in which God's people are threatened or menaced by enemy armies, and who turn to the Lord for relief.

Psalm 83

This psalm was written at a time when certain small nations and desert tribes around Israel had conspired together to wipe out Israel as a nation (vss. 2-5), and had persuaded Assyria to join them (v. 8). Apparently the main instigators of this coalition are "the children of Lot" (v. 8), i.e., Ammon and Moab (see *Genesis* 19:36-38), small nations located east of Jordan just south of Gilead (vss. 6, 7). They are joined by the nations of Edom directly south of Judah (v. 6), Philistia west of Judah in the south (v. 7), and Phoenicia (Tyre) west of Israel in the north (v. 7), and by the desert tribes of the Ishmaelites south of Judah (v. 6; see *Genesis* 25:16-18), the Hagrites (apparently descendants of Abraham's handmaid Hagar, see *Genesis* 16:10) who dwelt east of the Jordan in

Gilead (v. 6; see *I Chronicles* 5:10, 18-20) and near the Ishmaelites in the south, and Gebal located south of the Dead Sea near Petra in Edom (v. 7). This psalm gives the impression that Assyria is a formidable foe, but not a world power when it was composed. This would seem to place it roughly in the reigns of Jeroboam II of Israel (786-746 B. C., see *II Kings* 14:23-29) and Uzziah of Judah (783-742 B. C., see *II Kings* 15:1-7; *II Chronicles* 26) before Tiglath-pileser III made Assyria a great world power. However, other dates for the historical background of this psalm have been suggested all the way from the reign of Saul (1020-1000 B.C.) to the Maccabaean Age (167-76 B. C.), and there is not enough information in the text of the psalm itself to allow dogmatism on this matter.

Psalm 83 seems to fall naturally into three parts (vss. 1-8, 9-12, 13-18), each beginning with an appeal to God to intervene in behalf of his people and to give them relief from their enemies (vss. 1, 9, 13). The word "them" (referring to Israel) in the mouths of the enemy nations in v. 4 and the overall tenor of this psalm indicate that it was composed by a group of God's people, although the first person singular "my" in v. 13 may indicate that the king or a representative of the group was predominant in or at least had a certain role in its composition.

In the first paragraph (vss. 1-8), God's people beg him not to be silent (v. 1) because "his enemies" and "those who hate him" (v. 2) have risen up against his people. The enemies of God's people are God's enemies. Up until this time, the Israelites had been "God's protected ones" (v. 3). But now their foes have laid "crafty" plans and have "made a covenant" (v. 5) for the specific purpose of breaking through that protective wall and obliterating Israel.

"They say, 'Come, let us wipe them out as a nation;
  let the name of Israel be remembered no more!' " (v. 4).

The expression, "wiping out a nation's name," was commonly used in the ancient Near East to convey the idea of completely demolishing that nation. The prayer of this psalm is that God continue to "protect" his own.

In the second paragraph (vss. 9-12), the psalmists pray that God will overthrow their enemies as he had overthrown Israel's enemies in the past. Like the present foes (v. 4), they too had determined to decimate God's people.

"They said, 'Let us take possession for ourselves
of the pastures of God'." (v. 12).

Here the authors refer specifically to two events that took place in the period of the judges. One was the victory of Deborah and Barak over Jabin, king of Hazor, and his field general Sisera at the river Kishon (*Judges* 4-5; see especially 4:2, 6, 7, 13, 17, 23-24; 5:7, 12, 15, 19-21, 24-30) (vss. 9b-10). The reference to "En-dor" in v. 10 is puzzling, as no such place is mentioned in *Judges* 4-5. But it is located near Mount Tabor, which is mentioned several times in the account of Deborah's and Barak's victory (*Judges* 4:6, 12, 14). The other event mentioned in *Psalm* 83 was Gideon's victory over the Midianite nobles Oreb and Zeeb (*Judges* 7:25; 8:3), and the Midianite princes Zebah and Zalmunna (*Judges* 8:4-21) (vss. 9a, 11).

In the final paragraph (vss. 13-18), the singers give two reasons to induce God to overthrow those who plan to destroy his people. (1) God's victory would convince these enemies that he is superior to their gods, and thus they would forsake them to seek the name of the Lord, i.e., to accept him as the only true and living God (v. 16). (2) God's victory would convince these enemies that his rule is not limited to the people of Israel or the land of Israel, but that he *alone* is "the Most High over *all the earth*" (v. 18). Thus, these pleas for the defeat of Israel's enemies come from a concern for the salvation of all mankind. (On the problem of imprecations in the psalms, see Volume II, Lesson XIII).

This prayer that God would destroy Israel's enemies contains some graphic figures which the psalmists used to describe destruction. They compare it with whirling dust, chaff driven before the wind (v. 13), a raging forest fire (v. 14), and a hurricane (v. 15). The meaning of the Hebrew expression translated "whirling dust" in the RSV (v. 13) is variously understood. Some scholars think it means a tumbleweed (see the RSV footnote); and others, a wild artichoke plant or thistle that rolls up into a ball and is driven by the wind something like a tumbleweed.

Psalm 74

This psalm was composed shortly after the destruction of the temple (vss. 3, 7). Some scholars connect it with the desecration of the temple by Antiochus IV Epiphanes in 168 B. C., but it seems much more likely that it was composed shortly after the Babylonians destroyed Jerusalem (see "Mount Zion" in v. 2) and the temple in 587 B. C. The late date is usually supported by three arguments. (1) The "signs" that the invaders set up in the midst of the holy place (v. 4) are pagan religious symbols erected by Antiochus IV. However, this is by no means certain. It is just as possible that these "signs" are military symbols or "standards" (see *Numbers* 2:2) that were set up to indicate victory or possession. (2) Verse 8 refers to "synagogues" in the land, and there were no synagogues when the temple was destroyed in 587 B. C. Now while it is true that some English versions translate the ·Hebrew word here by "synagogues," this is not a necessary or a natural meaning in the present context. The psalmists are simply saying that not only did the enemy destroy the Jerusalem temple, but they also burned down the other "meeting places of God" or "sanctuaries" in the land. (3) This psalm comes from a time when God's people no longer have prophets to whom they can turn to learn God's plans and God's will (v. 8). Of course, it is true that this would fit Israel's situation at the beginning of the Maccabaean Age (see *I Maccabees* 4:46; 9:27; 14:41), but it also fits the period just after the destruction of the temple in 587 B.C. In fact, *Psalm* 74:8 probably means about the same thing as *Lamentations* 2:9:

> "Her (i.e., Jerusalem's) gates have sunk into the ground;
>   he (i.e., Babylon) has ruined and broken her bars;
> her king and princes are among the nations;
>   the law is no more,
> and her prophets obtain
>   no vision from the Lord." (See also *Ezekiel* 7:26).

The thought of *Psalm* 74:8 is not necessarily that there is no longer any prophet around Jerusalem, but that prophetic oracles which Israelite worshippers were accustomed to receiving as divine answers to their prayers had ceased. In addition to these considerations, it should also be pointed out that the references to the destruction of the woodwork and carvings of the temple fit the Babylonian demolition of the temple in 587 B. C. better than the desecration of the temple by Antiochus IV in 168 B. C.

This psalm was composed by a group of worshippers (note the first person plural "we" and "us" in vss. 1, 9) that had recently experienced the desecration and destruction of Jerusalem and the temple by the Babylonians. (The first person singular "my" in v. 12 may indicate that an individual who represented the sentiment of the group actually composed the psalm, or that each individual in the group distributively feels a personal commitment to the sentiment expressed by the group as a whole. If the former is true, the individual is hardly King Zedekiah, who was carried into exile, but he may have been the governor Gedaliah, a priest, a prophet, or a temple singer). Their prayer is composed of two parts, each of which is designed to induce God to intervene in behalf of his poor people (note especially vss. 19, 21) that are left in the land, and to give them relief from their foes. (1) They vividly describe the thoroughness of the destruction of Jerusalem and the temple (vss. 1-11). (2) They recall the mighty victories that God won over the enemies of chaos at creation, and emphasize how much more easily he could conquer these weaker enemies who have overthrown Zion (vss. 12-23).

In vss. 1-11, the poets acknowledge the destruction of Jerusalem and the temple as a demonstration of God's rejection of and anger against his people for their sins (v. 1). But they cannot believe that God could be satisfied with such a complete overthrow of his own people, desecration of his sanctuary, and decimation of his chosen city. One is struck by their emphasis on the *completeness* of the enemy destruction. God seems to have cast off his people "for ever" (v. 1), and the enemy seems to have the power to revile God's name "for ever" (v. 10). The ruins of Zion seem to be "perpetual," and the enemy has destroyed "everything" in the sanctuary (v. 3). They desecrated God's dwelling place "to the ground" (v. 7). They thought, "We will *utterly* destroy them," and they burned down "all" God's meeting places in the land (v. 8). Israel no longer has "any" prophet, and there is "none" among them that know how long the enemy will prevail (vss. 9-10).

In view of what appears to be a *complete* victory for the enemies of God's people, and a *complete* overthrow of Judah, the authors of this psalm give three reasons to move God to intervene in their behalf. (1) The people that these foes have overthrown are not just any people; they are the people whom God elected from all the peoples of the earth to be his own. They are "the sheep of his pasture" (v. 1), "his congregation," "the tribe of his heritage" that he had "redeemed" (v. 2), and they lived on Mount Zion, where God himself dwelt (v. 2). (2) These enemies are not simply Judah's enemies; they are God's enemies; and they have desecrated and destroyed that which belongs to and is precious to God. They roared in the midst of "his" holy place (v. 4); they set "his" sanctuary on fire; they desecrated the dwelling place of "his" holy name (v. 7); they burned down all "his" meeting places in the land (v. 8); and they continually revile "his" name (v. 10). (3) The enemy acted in pride and self-centeredness. They "roared" like a lion in the midst of God's holy place, and set up "their own" signs (v. 4). They said, "*We* will utterly subdue them" (v. 8). They "scoff at" and "revile" God's name (v. 10; see also vss. 18, 22-23). Surely God cannot and will not tolerate such arrogance!

It is interesting that questions beginning with the word "Why" stand at the beginning and the end of this paragraph (twice each in vss. 1 and 11). In v. 1 the worshippers ask "why" God has cast off his own people, and in v. 11 they ask "why" he does not intervene and devour their enemies. The figure of God keeping his right hand in his bosom in v. 11 calls to mind the sign in which Moses put his hand into his bosom (i.e., the folds of his robe) and brought it out leprous, then put it back into his bosom and brought it out clean (see *Exodus* 4:6-7). The context shows that the word "signs" has a different meaning in v. 9 from what it does in v. 4. In v. 4 it refers to military standards or symbols that were set up by the invading army to claim their victory over and possession of Jerusalem and the temple, but in v. 11 it refers to indications of God's presence among his people, as through prophetic oracles.

In vss. 12-23, the psalmists state four reasons why God should intervene to deliver his people and overthrow their enemies, some of which are identical with the reasons given in vss. 1-11. (1) Historically, even beginning with the creation of the world, God has continually "worked salvation" in the midst of the earth, and not destruction (vss. 12-17). He is the great "king" over all the earth (v. 12). In keeping with his character, he should bring salvation to his people now. In their description of creation, these poets borrow mythological language from Babylonian and Ugaritic (Syrian) religions. According to Babylonian mythology, the god Marduk divided in two the dragon Tiamat (symbolized by the ocean of chaos), and created the universe from her carcass. According to Ugaritic mythology, the god Baal broke the seven-headed monster Lotan (Hebrew Leviathan) with a magic club. The authors of *Psalm* 74 affirm that it was Yahweh or the Lord (not Marduk or Baal) who created the world. It was he who "divided the sea," who "broke the heads of the dragons on the waters" (v. 13), and who "crushed the heads of Leviathan" and "gave him as food for the creatures of the wilderness" (v. 14); in other words, it was he who brought order out of chaos (see *Genesis* 1:1-2). He made the waters covering the earth recede, caused the dry land to appear, and made the various waterways on earth (v. 15). He made the sun and moon as luminaries for the day and the night (v. 16), and established the seasons, "summer and winter" (v. 17). It is not surprising to find these poets borrowing language from neighboring peoples to convey truths about God, because this is done elsewhere in the Old Testament (see e.g., *Psalm* 89:9-12; *Isaiah* 14:12-14; 51:9-11) and in the New (see Paul's quotations from pagan authors in *Acts* 17:28; *I Corinthians* 15:33; and *Titus* 1:12).

(2) Israel's enemies do not simply scoff at and revile Israel; they scoff at and revile God's name (vss. 18, 22-23). (3) God's people are wholly destitute and helpless. They are "downtrodden," "poor, " and "needy" (vss. 19, 21). Surely God cannot turn a deaf ear to the cries of those who are in such miserable circumstances! (4) These who are persecuted are not just any people; they are God's "dove" (v. 19), the people with whom he has made "his covenant" (v. 20). How can God turn his back on his own?

Of the several terms and expressions that are repeated in *Psalm* 74, two call for brief comment. (a) Six times the psalmists plead with God to "remember" or "not to forget" his relationship to his people and the behavior of the enemy.

> "Remember thy congregation" (v. 2).
> "Remember Mount Zion" (v. 2).
> "Remember . . . how the enemy scoffs" (v. 18).
> "Do not forget the life of thy poor" (v. 19).
> "Remember how the impious scoff at thee" (v. 22).
> "Do not forget the clamor of thy foes" (v. 23).

One should not conclude from these statements that God would forget such things. Rather, they are the kind of expressions that seem to come to mind naturally when one is appealing for help in desperate circumstances. (b) The term "for ever" occurs three times in this psalm (vss. 1, 10, 19). In each case, the poets are pleading with God not to allow present terrible conditions to continue on and on. Since the authors of this psalm knew when they composed it that they (vss. 1, 19) and their enemies (v. 10) would die, "for ever" does not mean "eternally (of time)," but "as long as they (or their enemies) shall live."

REVIEW QUESTIONS

1. Describe and discuss the historical background of *Psalm* 83. Study especially vss. 2-8.

2. Give a three point outline of *Psalm* 83, then tell in your own words the content of this psalm.

3. Study carefully the statements made by the enemies of the authors of *Psalm* 83 in vss. 4 and 12. What do you learn about their attitude from these statements? Do you feel that people today have similar attitudes toward and designs on the church? Discuss at length.

4. The authors of *Psalm* 83 urged God to overthrow their enemies as he had overthrown Israel's enemies in the past. What two specific events in Israel's past does he mention? Tell each event in detail on the basis of your own study of *Judges* 4-5 and 8.

5. What figures do the poets of *Psalm* 83 use to describe the destruction that they hope God will bring on their enemies? Verses 13-15.

6. Describe and discuss the historical background of *Psalm* 74. What two major views are given as to the precise setting for this psalm? What arguments support each view? Study as many commentaries and other works as you can find to discover other views on the historical background of this psalm. Which historical situation do you feel lies behind it? Why?

7. Name at least four reasons given by the authors of *Psalm* 74 to move God to answer their prayer, and to deliver them from their enemies. Do you think Christians should use such arguments to induce God to answer their prayers? Why?

8. Study carefully *Psalm* 74:12-17. How do you explain vss. 13-14 in particular? What are the "dragons" and what is "Leviathan?" Do you think it was all right for biblical writers to borrow terminology from and to quote from their pagan neighbors? Discuss at length. When they did this, did they mean the same thing that their neighbors did? Discuss.

9. Discuss the phrases beginning with "Remember" and "Do not forget" in *Psalm* 74:2 (twice), 18, 19, 22, 23. Do you feel that a Christian can appeal to God to "remember" his people or the behavior of his enemies? Discuss.

10. Discuss the meaning of the term "for ever" in *Psalm* 74:1, 10, 19. Do you think it means "eternally?" Why? What do you think it means? Support your position with good arguments.

Lesson V

THE VICTIMIZED FIND STABILITY IN GOD (I)

*"I look to the right and watch,
but there is none who takes notice of me;
no refuge remains to me,
no man cares for me.
I cry to thee, O Lord;
I say, 'Thou art my refuge,
my portion in the land of the living'." (Psalm 142:4-5).*

Because of their honesty and integrity, God's people are vulnerable to the selfish and malicious schemes of worldly men and religious charlatans and hucksters. This does not necessarily mean that the child of God is naive or stupid. But since his disposition is to think well of all men, he constantly stands in danger of being victimized by those who do not have God at the center of their lives. That this is a major problem in the daily life of God's servant is emphasized, among other things, by the many psalms that deal with this issue. The next two lessons call attention to some of these.

Psalm 55

Some scholars have argued that *Psalm* 55 was originally two independent psalms which later came to be combined. However, those who take this view cannot agree on the verses to be included in each of the original psalms. It seems best to take *Psalm* 55 as a unit. The somewhat irregular flow of thought may be due to the complexity of the poet's problem, and to his emotional involvement in it.

Apparently the author of *Psalm* 55 was living in the city of Jerusalem when he composed this psalm. He refers to a "city" (v. 9) surrounded by "walls" (v. 10), in which God's "house" (the temple) was located (v. 14). The psalmist and his friends (v. 20) are oppressed by a large number of wicked men (vss. 3, 11, 18). Evidently they are a well-organized band of ruffians, who carefully plan deeds of violence and strife in the city (v. 9), who continually roam the city walls in search for opportunities to cause mischief and trouble (v. 10), and who practice oppression and fraud in the marketplace (vss. 11, 23). If the city intended here is Jerusalem, these wicked men must be "God's people." Unfortunately, every generation of God's people has included people of this character. But the situation is even worse! The poet's best friend, his "equal," his "companion," his "familiar friend" (vss. 13, 20), had betrayed him and his comrades, and had broken their covenant of friendship by casting his lot with malicious oppressors (v. 20). The psalmist can remember when they had conversed together on the most intimate matter, when they had enjoyed each other's fellowship in God's house (v. 14). But now he realizes that all this show of friendship and loyalty was nothing but a sham. His friend was using an external show of religion and of communion to promote his own selfish goals of personal gain, and thus he would not hesitate to betray his friend's confidence in him if this was to his best interest. As the poet reflects on this man's true character, he says sadly:

"His speech was smoother than butter,
  yet war was in his heart,
 his words were softer than oil,
  yet they were drawn swords." (v. 21).

Of all people, a man should be able to open his heart fully to his Christian brother, but unfortunately there are those even in the church who do not hesitate to betray a brother's confidence to promote their own quirks and interests, just as the psalmist's best friend had done.

This psalm falls into two parts. (1) The author begs God to intervene and save him from his enemies who plot his destruction (vss. 1-11). (2) He expresses his confidence that

God will deliver him from the schemes of the man who had been his best friend, but who had recently betrayed him (vss. 12–23).

In vss. 1–11, the poet begins by pleading with God to hear his prayer (vss. 1-2a). He describes his terrible plight in order to induce God to intercede (vss. 2b-5). The meaning of the phrase "terrors of death" (v. 4) is hard to determine. If v. 15 is understood as an imprecatory prayer that God would punish the psalmist's enemies as they had intended to treat him, then it is likely this expression in v. 4 means that they sought to kill him. This interpretation might be supported by his reference to his enemies as "men of blood" (v. 23). However, the means by which they intend to kill him are still obscure. Are they planning to ambush him and actually murder him with their own hands? Or are they falsely accusing him of a capital crime before the elders of the city? The allusions to their false speech (vss. 9, 21) could argue in favor of the latter, but this is by no means certain.

The poet's problems are so devastating that he longs to go out into the wilderness to get away from it all. His words beautifully capture the innermost feelings of many a troubled soul in every age:

> "O that I had wings like a dove!
>   I would fly away and be at rest;
> yea, I would wander afar,
>   I would lodge in the wilderness,
> I would haste to find me a shelter
>   from the raging wind and tempest." (vss. 6-8).

But physical escape is impossible under the present circumstances. And so the psalmist turns to God, and begs him to overthrow the plans of these violent and treacherous men (vss. 9-11).

In vss. 12-23, the author voices the deepest hurt that a man can suffer—his best friend has proved to be a fraud, and has betrayed their intimate relationship. He could bear to be victimized by an "enemy" or an "adversary" (v. 12), but for his own "familiar friend" and "companion" to betray his trust was more than he could take (v. 13). Time and again they had shared sweet communion and fellowship with one another and with God in the temple (v. 14), and it seems unthinkable that his comrade could turn against him, bring accusations against him, and plot to have him put to death. One would like to think that such things *could not possibly* plague the fellowship of Christians, but the church in every age is plagued with such ungodly conduct.

Feeling the full weight of this crushing betrayal, the psalmist declares confidently that God will cast his enemies into the grave (vss. 15, 19, 23), and unburdens his heart fully to the Lord, who never betrays a man's confidence (vss. 16-19). The identity of the speaker in v. 22 is uncertain. The psalmist may be talking to himself, or this verse may contain the assuring words of a cult prophet or a temple priest in response to the author's prayers. Taken either way, this verse contains a most fitting solution to the poet's complex problem:

"Cast your burden on the Lord,
  and he will sustain you;
he will never permit
  the righteous to be moved."

Psalm 94

This psalm was written by a very sensitive person who saw clearly the difference between those who truly humbled themselves before God and those who used their religious masquerade as a front for all sorts of selfish ambitions. He makes a sharp distinction between the genuine people of God, who are constantly aware of God's intervention into men's lives (vss. 9-10, 14, 19) and who sympathize with and strive to help the oppressed (vss. 5-6), and those who profess to be God's people, but who do not believe that God continues to work in human life (vss. 7-11) and who crush the helpless (vss. 5-6, 20-21). A similar distinction between the true and the false among God's own people appears in Micah 2:8-9, which should be studied carefully in connection with this psalm. The poet identifies himself with the afflicted. He has the same problems that they have, and his heart goes out to them. Their enemies are "wicked rulers" who use their authority to make laws and statutes that hurt the poor and help the rich (v. 20). They arrange for charges to be brought against the poor, have them brought into court, engineer false charges against them, and sentence them to death (v. 21; see the obvious implications of such practices in vss. 15, 16). Then they boast of their accomplishments, and give an arrogant air wherever they go (vss. 2-4). These are not foreigners, but members of God's chosen people, at least by reputation and outward show (vss. 7, 8). Yet, in God's eyes those whom they oppress are the true people of God (vss. 5, 14). In view of this analysis, it is not necessary to divide this song into two originally independent psalms, the first being a national lament, and the second an individual lament, as some scholars do.

Psalm 94, then, may be divided easily into two parts. (1) The psalmist urges God to relieve his true people from their affliction by bringing their oppressors to justice (vss. 1-7), rebukes these oppressors for thinking that God ignores their evil deeds and will never bring them to justice (vss. 8-11), and pronounces a blessing on the true Israelite who accepts and benefits from God's teaching through chastening (vss. 12-15) (vss. 1-15). (2) On the basis of his own personal experiences in the past (vss. 16-19), he expresses his confidence that God will bring those who oppress him and his fellow-sufferers to justice, and will deliver the innocent (vss. 20-23) (vss. 16-23).

In vss. 1-15, the poet begins by pleading with God to humble the proud oppressors of his helpless people (vss. 1-7), especially the "widow," "sojourner," and "fatherless" (v. 6). This concern for widows, orphans, and strangers is basic to true religion, as is emphasized in both Old (*Exodus* 22:21-22; *Deuteronomy* 10:18; *Isaiah* 1:16-17; *Jeremiah* 7:5-7; etc.) and New Testaments (*I John* 3:17-18; *James* 1:26-27). That God is a "God of vengeance" (v. 1) is not to be taken to mean that at heart he is a "vengeful God," but rather that (as "judge of the earth") he is a God who rights the wrongs that unjust men bring upon the helpless (v. 2). Their arrogance and boasting are particularly repulsive (vss. 2-4). They are cocksure that their ungodly plans will succeed, not only because they are in positions of leadership over God's people who cannot and would not dare retaliate, but also because they are confident that God ignores the attitudes and behavior of his own chosen people. They affirm:

> "The Lord does not see;
>   the God of Jacob does not perceive." (v. 7).

The psalmist addresses these oppressors directly (vss. 8-11). He calls them the "dullest" of the people and "fools." And yet they purported to be the leaders of God's people (see v. 20). Is it not true that God is the one who gives man ears with which to hear and eyes with which to see? (See *Exodus* 4:11). Then surely he can hear men's evil plots and see their evil deeds against his genuine people! (v. 9). Is it not true that God chastens the nations when they sin, and that he is the one responsible for men having the ability to learn and know? Then surely he will chasten those of his own people that sin, and surely he knows the motives of his own people (vss. 10-11). The thought here is powerful and much needed in the modern church. He who gives life and sustains life must himself be alive! He who made ears and eyes and minds can certainly hear and see and know! The notion that God ceased working in his world at some time in the past is the same sort of practical atheism reflected by the psalmist's oppressors in *Psalm* 94.

Now the psalmist pronounces a blessing on the true servant of God, who accepts God's chastening as a means of improving his life and service to the Lord (vss. 12-15). Such chastening prepares the godly for additional troubles that are bound to come later in life (v. 13; see the similar thought of Paul in *Philippians* 4:10-13), and assures him that suffering is temporary, for "the Lord will not forsake his people" (v. 14; see *Deuteronomy* 31:6; *Joshua* 1:5; *I Samuel* 12:22; *Romans* 11:1-2).

In vss. 16-23, the author describes his own afflictions and, on the basis of former experiences, expresses his confidence that God will deliver him and overthrow his oppressors. When evildoers afflict him, no one is brave enough to defend him (v. 16). And yet all is not lost! He would already be in the grave ("the land of silence;" see *Psalm* 115:17) if God had not intervened on previous occasions to help him (v. 17). The Lord's "steadfast love" sustained him (v. 18), and the Lord's "consolations" cause him to rejoice (v. 19). Thus, he has claimed the Lord as his "stronghold" and "the rock of his refuge" (v. 22), i.e., he seeks protection from his oppressors in God alone. In this advantageous position, he is confident that no matter how powerful and well-organized his enemies may be (vss. 20-21), God will punish them for their malicious attacks on the helpless of his people (v. 23).

REVIEW QUESTIONS

1. Describe the afflictions encountered by the author of *Psalm* 55. Have you ever had an intimate friend betray you or try to hurt you? Was this friend a professed Christian? Share your experience with the class. Discuss this problem in the church in detail.

2. Give a two point outline of *Psalm* 55, then tell the content of this psalm in your own words.

3. Read *Psalm* 55:6-8 carefully. Have you ever wanted to run away from all your problems, to get away from it all? How does one face a situation in which he feels himself trapped and from which he cannot escape?

4. Study *Psalm* 55:22 carefully. Discuss practical ways in which this verse can give encouragement to the child of God who is burdened with a multiplicity of heavy problems.

5. Read *Psalm* 94:5, 8, 14 carefully. Discuss the two ways in which the idea of the "people of God" is used in these verses. What important lesson can the modern church learn from this distinction? According to *Psalm* 94, on the basis of what two things is this distinction made? Discuss.

6. Give a two point outline of *Psalm* 94, then tell in your own words the content of this psalm.

7. Read carefully *Psalm* 94:7-11. Do you believe that God is responsible for your ability to hear, see, and think? Discuss in detail. Is it logical to believe that God could give us the ability to hear, see, and think without being able to hear, see, and think himself? Do you believe that God knows what you think and sees what you do and hears what you say? Do you believe he works in your life? Discuss.

8. According to *Psalm* 94:12-15, what two lessons can a servant of God learn from his afflictions? Discuss the practical applications of this in detail.

Lesson VI

THE VICTIMIZED FIND STABILITY IN GOD (II)

"I am for peace;
but when I speak,
they are for war!" (Psalm 120:7).

Psalm 71

The author of *Psalm* 71 is an old man (vss. 9, 18) who had served God ever since he could remember ("from my youth," vss. 5, 17; "from my birth," v. 6; "from my mother's womb," v. 6). He had been through many hard times, but God had delivered him again and again (vss. 17, 20). Now he is confronted with new problems. His wicked enemies are convinced that he is vulnerable now (vss. 4, 13, 24). As an old man, and possibly sick, he no longer has the strength to resist his adversaries as he once did (v. 9), and they use this against him as an indication that God has forsaken him, making him easy prey (vss. 10-11). The many strong requests throughout the psalm indicate that the poet feels that his situation is desperate: "Deliver me" (v. 2); "Rescue me" (vss. 2, 4; see v. 23); "Do not cast me off" (v. 9); "Forsake me not" (vss. 9, 18); "Be not far from me" (v. 12); "Make haste to help me" (v. 12). Apparently this author was a temple singer, who frequently praised God for his wonderful works (vss. 6, 8, 14-18, 22-24) to the accompaniment of the harp and the lyre (v. 22).

The psalmist's promises to "praise" God when he is delivered from his enemies come at the end of each section (especially vss. 8, 15-16, 22-24), and these seem to divide the psalm naturally into three paragraphs of eight verses each. (1) The poet urges God to rescue him from unjust and cruel men because he has put his trust in God from his youth up (vss. 1-8). (2) He tells God that his accusers have concluded from his miserable circumstances that the Lord has forsaken him, and he begs God to prove that this is not the case in order that he might again praise him (vss. 9-16). (3) He expresses his confidence that God will save him in this trial as he had done so many times before (vss. 17-24). Throughout the psalm, the poet appeals, not to his own goodness or merits, but to God's "righteousness" (vss. 2, 15, 16, 19, 24), which apparently has reference to his "deeds of salvation" or "mighty deeds" or the "great things" he did for his people, in particular the psalmist himself (as the synonymous parallelism in vss. 15, 16, and 19 respectively indicate).

In vss. 1-8, the author indicates that he is in the clutches of those who are "wicked," "unjust," and "cruel" (v. 4). Many view him as a "portent" (v. 7), i.e., as the object of God's wrath. But he "hopes" and "trusts" in God (v. 5), as his "refuge" (vss. 1, 3, 7), to protect him from those who are determined to destroy him. As might be expected from an old temple singer and musician, many of his statements apparently are borrowed from familiar lines that he had often heard and sung in the worship. Verses 1-3 are almost identical with *Psalm* 31:1-3; vss. 5-6 are similar to 22:9-10; v. 12 to 22:11 and 70:1; v. 15 to 40:5; and v. 19 to 86:8. He has served God from his youth (vss. 5-6), and has not been disappointed; therefore, even in his distresses he "praises" God "all the day" (v. 8; "continually," v. 6). "All the day" is an important term in this psalm, as the author uses it again in vss. 15 and 24.

In vss. 9-16, the poet pleads with God to deliver him because he is old and has no strength to help himself (v. 9). His enemies have concluded from his pitiable condition that God has forsaken him, and therefore he is vulnerable to their attacks (vss. 10-11). Thus, he begs God to help him (v. 12) and to put his accusers to shame (v. 13). When this happens, he promises to praise God "alone" (v. 16) "yet more and more" (v. 14), and to tell others of his righteous acts "all the day" (v. 15). How important it is for God's people to openly declare what God has done for them!

In vss. 17-24, the psalmist declares that God had taught him from his youth to bear his trials by unshaken trust in him (vss. 17, 20), and that God had never disappointed him, as is evidenced from the fact that he "still" proclaims God's wondrous deeds (v. 17). Now that he is old, he pleads with God not to forsake him (v. 18), for he wishes to continue to tell others what God has done for him (vss. 18-19). Then with renewed confidence, he affirms with conviction that God will "revive him again" (v. 20) in the present crisis, and then he will again praise God with the harp and lyre (v. 22), because he has put his enemies to shame (v. 24).

Psalm 109

The key to a correct understanding of this psalm is the interpretation of vss. 6-19. Whereas the psalmist speaks of his enemies in the plural in vss. 1-5 and 20-31, the object of the accusations and curses in vss. 6-19 is singular. Scholars have explained this in three ways. (1) Some think that the psalmist is still speaking of the group that opposes him in vss. 6-19, but that he either views them distributively (i.e., he has in mind each individual member of the group), or he thinks of them collectively as if they were one man, perhaps because they work together so well to try to destroy him. (2) Others believe that in vss. 6-19 he devotes himself wholly to the leader of his accusers, because he had been so prominent in spearheading the attack against him. (3) It seems best to think that in vss. 6-19 the author is quoting the curses, charges, and attacks brought against him by his enemies. Then he replies to these in vss. 20-31.

A couple of technical matters must be treated in order to correctly interpret this psalm. (1) The Hebrew word translated "accuser" in the RSV of v. 6 is *satan*, and some English versions actually read "Satan" here. This is the same Hebrew word rendered "Satan" in *Job* 1:6-9, 12; 2:1-4, 6; *I Chronicles* 21:1; and *Zechariah* 3:1-2. However, it is clear from the context of *Psalm* 109 that the psalmist is not referring to "the devil," but to a "wicked *man*" (note the synonymous parallelism in v. 6) who had been selected by the poet's enemies to bring false charges against him in court. As a matter of fact, it was probably from this use of the word "satan" in Israelite court life that the expression came to be applied to the superhuman spiritual being that the Bible calls the devil. Perhaps an important lesson can be learned here concerning the method to be used in interpreting difficult biblical texts and concepts, as well as the proper method to be used in communicating the biblical message to lost mankind in modern times! The inspired speakers and writers of Old and New Testament times used terms and ideas that were *already familiar* to their audiences, and used them as vehicles to convey truths concerning the spiritual realm that lay beyond man's daily experiences. Thus, in order to explain the nature and work of "the devil," they used the word "satan," which their audiences *already understood* as a man who brought accusations (probably usually *false* accusations) against defendants in court trials. Christian preachers and teachers today should strive to use terms already familiar to their audiences as vehicles of communicating the good news of Christ.

(2) In the RSV, v. 16 reads:

"For he did not remember to show kindness,
  but pursued the poor and needy
  and the brokenhearted to *their* death."

The word "their" gives the impression that the psalmist's enemies are accusing him of being responsible for the deaths of *several* "poor and needy" people. This is an unfortunate rendering, because the Hebrew is clearly singular at this point. The poet's enemies are charging him specifically with the death of an individual who was poor and needy, and they are hoping that the court will find him "guilty" (v. 7). It is in direct response to this charge that the author prays in v. 27 that God might make it clear to the court and to his accusers that the deceased died a natural death, i.e., that it was God and not the psalmist who was responsible for his death. This is what he means when he prays:

"Let them know that *this* is thy hand;
   thou, O Lord, hast done *it*!"

With these matters clarified, it seems natural to divide *Psalm* 109 into three parts. (1) The poet describes the serious situation in which he finds himself. He is on trial for something he did not do; his accusers are bringing false charges against him (vss. 1-5). (2) He rehearses the accusations and the curses that his enemies have brought against him (vss. 6-19). (3) He begs God to turn these curses back upon the heads of those who have levelled them against him and to show him innocent; then he will praise the Lord as one who clears the falsely accused (vss. 20-31).

In vss. 1-5, the author begs God not to be silent (v. 1), because he is being falsely accused (note "deceitful mouths," "lying tongues," in v. 2; "without cause," in v. 3). And to make matters worse, those who are bringing these accusations are people to whom he has demonstrated his love, to whom he had done good, and for whom he has prayed (vss. 4-5). In exchange for his love, they have only hatred (vss. 3, 5); they reward him evil for good (v. 5). The sin of returning evil for good (see *Psalm* 38:20; *I Samuel* 24:17), and the importance of returning good for evil (see *Exodus* 23:4-5; *Proverbs* 25:21-22), are emphasized in the Old Testament, as they are in the New (see e.g., *Matthew* 5:38-48; *Romans* 12:19-21, *I Peter* 2:18-25).

In vss. 6-19, the psalmist recites the "words of hate" (see v. 3) that his accusers have brought against him. They have decided to set up a wicked man (an "accuser," a "satan") to testify against him in court (v. 6), in hopes that the elders of the city might render a "guilty" verdict against him (v. 7). The specific charge is that he used "black magic" to bring death on a "poor and needy" man (vss. 16-17). In court, the "accuser" tries to make him appear like a sorcerer who "loved to curse" and not to bless (v. 17), who "clothed himself with cursing as his coat" (v. 18). Having characterized him as one who loved to work "black magic," the accuser prays before the court that he might be cursed himself. He cries:

"May it (i.e., cursing) soak into his body like water,
  like oil into his bones!
May it be like a garment which he wraps round him,
  like a belt with which he daily girds himself!"
                                        (vss. 18-19).

All this is designed to persuade the judges to declare him
guilty of murder. If this is achieved, then the psalmist will
receive the death penalty. So his opponents pray that his
days be few, that his hard earned possessions fall into the
hands of others (vss. 8, 11), that his children become orphans
and his wife a widow (vss. 9-10, 12), that his ancestors be
abased and his mother be put to shame (v. 14), and that his
good name be cut off for ever (vss. 13, 15).

In response to these hateful and degrading curses, the
psalmist prays that God will render to his adversaries what
they intended to bring upon him, and that he will deliver him
from the false charges brought against him by revealing the
truth to the court and to his accusers (vss. 20-31). The word
"this" in the statement, "May *this* be the reward of my
accusers from the Lord" (v. 20), refers back to the curses
brought against the psalmist by his enemies in vss. 6-19. The
words "this" and "it" in the statement,

"Let them know that *this* is thy hand;
  thou, O Lord, hast done *it*!" (v. 27),

refers back to the enemies' accusation that he had murdered
a "poor and needy" man (v. 16). His enemies had prayed that
his "curse" upon the deceased might be like a garment that
he wraps about him every day (v. 19), and in fitting response
he cries:

"May my accusers be *clothed* with dishonor;
  may they be *wrapped* in their own shame *as in a
  mantle*!"
                                        (v. 29).

They had hoped that he would be found "guilty" and be
given the death sentence (vss. 7-8), but he expresses his

assurance that God will "save him from those who condemn him to death." (v. 31).

The psalmist gives three reasons why God should intervene in his behalf. (a) God's fundamental character is "steadfast love." Since the psalmist is not guilty of the crime of which he is accused, he pleads with God to demonstrate this steadfast love by showing that he is not guilty (vss. 21, 26). (b) The psalmist has prayed and fasted for many days, and now he is very weak and looks bad (vss. 23-24). His enemies have used his appearance as a proof that God is already punishing him for his crime (v. 25). The truth is that, like the man he is supposed to have killed by black magic (v. 16), he also is one of the "poor and needy" (v. 22). And now he is being blamed for a natural death (v. 27). (c) If and when God delivers him, the psalmist promises to praise him among the people as one who "stands at the right hand of the needy" (vss. 30-31), i.e., as defender of the falsely accused and innocent.

REVIEW QUESTIONS

1. Describe the problems faced by the author of *Psalm* 71. Indicate the kind of man he was. Do you know people today in similar circumstances? Share your insights with the class.

2. List the phrases used by the poet of *Psalm* 71 indicating his desperate situation. Discuss the significance of each of these.

3. Give a three point outline of *Psalm* 71, then state in your own words the content of this psalm.

4. Read carefully *Psalm* 71:2, 15, 16, 19, 24. In light of the synonymous parallelism in some of these verses, what is meant by God's "righteousness," "righteous acts," or "righteous help?" Discuss the significance of this in daily living.

5. Study *Psalm 109:6-19* carefully. State three views as to the speakers and significance of this paragraph. What is the view of the author of this booklet? Do you agree? Why?

6. Discuss the word "accuser" in *Psalm* 109:6. What is the Hebrew word lying behind this? In what other Old Testament passages does this word occur? How does a knowledge of the Hebrew word here help us understand how to communicate the gospel to lost mankind? Discuss the principle suggested here.

7. Discuss the meaning of *Psalm* 109:16, and the connection between this verse and v. 27. What was the main accusation that this psalmist's accusers were bringing against him? What was the penalty that they were hoping the court would bring against the poet?

8. How was the author of *Psalm* 109 treating his enemies? See especially vss. 4-5. What other passages in the Old and New Testaments teach this same principle? Discuss its importance in godly living.

9. Give a three point outline of *Psalm* 109, then tell in your own words the content of this psalm.

10. What three reasons does the author of *Psalm* 109 give to induce God to answer his pleas? See especially vss. 21-31. Should a Christian try to persuade God to answer his prayers by giving similar inducements? Discuss at length.

Lesson VII

THE GREAT SEARCHER OF HEARTS

"The heart is deceitful above all things,
and desperately corrupt;
who can understand it?
'I the Lord search the mind
and try the heart,
to give to every man according to his ways,
according to the fruit of his doings.' " (Jeremiah 17:9-10).

Volume II, Lessons VIII-XIII, and Volume III, Lessons I-VI, have dealt with psalms in which men come before God in worship with a variety of moods for a variety of reasons. A number of other psalms fall within this group. However, attention is now turned to certain psalms which in one way or other teach important spiritual lessons. Some scholars call at least some of these Wisdom Psalms, because they are similar in some ways to Wisdom Literature, like Job, Proverbs, and Ecclesiastes. For the purpose of the present series of lessons, this category of psalms is defined much more freely or flexibly than is normally the case in scholarly studies. The present lesson deals with three psalms which depict God as the searcher of human hearts.

Psalm 7

The author of *Psalm* 7 has been accused of betraying his friend and of stealing possessions from his enemy (vss. 3-4). His accusers are as vicious as lions (vss. 2, 6), and have carefully laid a shrewd plan to destroy the psalmist (vss. 14-16). Apparently he comes before the ark of the covenant in the Jerusalem temple, and prays to God to deliver him from his enemies (vss. 1, 6, 9, 15-16), and to show that he is innocent (vss. 3-4, 8-10). The imperatives "Arise, O Lord," "Lift thyself up," and "Awake, O my God" (v. 6), recall the formula that Moses used when the ark set out from the camp before Israel's armies as they went into battle against their enemies (*Numbers* 10:35). Perhaps the poet sees a parallel between Israel and her enemies on the one hand, and himself and his enemies on the other. Furthermore, "Take thy seat on high" (v. 7; if this is the correct reading) reflects the Old Testament idea that the ark is the throne-chariot of the Lord, above which he sits enthroned as king (see *I Samuel* 4:4; *II Samuel* 6:2).

Psalm 7 seems to fall naturally into three divisions. (1) The psalmist asks God to deliver him from his accusers and affirms his innocence (vss. 1-5). (2) He pleads with God, as the righteous judge who tries men's hearts, to examine his heart and the hearts of his enemies, and to act accordingly (vss. 6-16). (3) He promises to praise the Lord for his righteous judgment (v. 17).

In vss. 1-5, the poet claims God as his protection ("refuge") from his vicious pursuers who seek to destroy him as a lion rends its prey (vss. 1-2). He seeks to prove his innocence by asking God to let his enemies destroy him if he is guilty of the treachery and theft of which they have accused him (vss. 3-5). This type of affirmation of innocence also appears in Solomon's dedication of the temple (*I Kings* 8:31-32) and Job's speech of vindication (*Job* 31).

In vss. 6-16, the poet prays that God would rise up as the mighty king of the nations who "judges the peoples" (v. 8), and vindicate him "according to the integrity that is in him" (v. 8), i.e., in keeping with his actions and motivations. Unlike human judges, the Lord "tries the minds and hearts" (v. 9); in other words, he knows whether a man really is what he claims to be. On this basis, he "saves the upright in heart" (v. 10). If a man is not genuine, he demands that he "repent" (v. 12), and if he does not he punishes him according to his iniquity (vss. 15-16). That God is concerned about man's motives and continually searches his heart is a truth that permeates the Old Testament (see e.g., *Jeremiah* 4:4; 9:25-26) and the New (see e.g., *Romans* 2:28-29).

Verse 14 gives a vivid description of the progressive nature of sin:

> "Behold, the wicked man *conceives* evil,
>   and *is pregnant* with mischief,
>   and *brings forth* lies."

The movement from temptation to the decision to commit sin to the overt act of sin itself is compared with the natural progression from conception to the pregnancy to birth. A very similar picture is given in *James* 1:14-15:

> "Each person is tempted when he is *lured and enticed* by his own desire. Then desire when it has *conceived gives birth to* sin; and sin when it is full-grown *brings forth* death."

Psalm 26

The author of this psalm has been falsely accused of some crime, and he begs God to "vindicate" him (v. 1) that he might not be destroyed like the guilty (vss. 9-10). He gives four proofs of his innocence, and these divide the psalm into four parts. (1) He is not afraid for God to examine his heart to see whether he really is what he claims to be (vss. 1-3). (2) He has scrupulously avoided participating in the affairs of "false men" (vss. 4-5). (3) He has meticulously subjected himself to the rite of purification which is demanded of one accused of his crime (vss. 6-7). (4) He genuinely loves the temple, where God is present, and where God's people assemble to worship him (vss. 8-12). It is significant that the psalm begins and ends with the affirmation, "I walk in my integrity" (vss. 1, 11).

In vss. 1-3, the poet declares his innocence on the basis of his unwavering trust in God's steadfast love and faithfulness. His has not been .a self-centered life, but a life centered in God. But he realizes that this profession could be taken as a mere external claim. So he asks:

> "Prove me, O Lord, and try me;
>   test my heart and my mind." (v. 2).

God is the great searcher of hearts, and the psalmist longs for God to search his heart in order to prove that he is a man of integrity and thus vindicate him.

In vss. 4-5, the author acknowledges that there are those who claim to be good men when really their hearts are evil ("false men"). But he has avoided their fellowship in order that he might not be tainted with their insincerity (see *Proverbs* 4:14-17; *I Corinthians* 15:33).

In vss. 6-7, the psalmist declares that he has performed the ritual acts in the temple prescribed for one accused of his crime. He has washed his hands, which was a common symbolic act indicating innocence (see *Deuteronomy* 21:6-7; *Psalm* 73:13; *Matthew* 27:24). He has gone around the altar with the procession (see *Psalm* 118:27), and has declared God's wondrous deeds to others.

In vss. 8-12, the poet proclaims his genuine love for the temple, where God's glory (i.e., the ark, see *I Samuel* 4:17-22, especially vss. 21-22; *Psalm* 78:60-61) dwells (v. 8), and where God's people assemble for worship (v. 12). Since he has not committed the sins of wicked men, he prays that he will not suffer the fate of evil men (vss. 9-10). Instead, he begs God to "redeem" him (v. 11), i.e., to save him from the death penalty that his accusers are seeking.

Psalm 139

This is one of the most beautiful and spiritually profound treasures of the Psalter. There is no agreement among scholars concerning the situation lying behind it. However, it seems likely that the psalmist is under attack by "men of blood" (v. 19), who "hate" God (v. 21), "maliciously defy" him, and "lift themselves up" (v. 20) or "rise up" against him (v. 21). Now "men of blood" could mean men who seek to murder the poet. But it seems more likely that they have brought accusations against him, and hope that he will receive the death penalty in court. Assuming that the entire psalm is directed to this problem, it may be implied from v. 2 that they had accused him of certain deeds that he had not done, and from v. 4 that they had interpreted things that he had said in ways which he never intended. And the whole tenor of the psalm indicates that their ultimate goal is to separate the psalmist from God (see especially vss. 7-12). The psalm falls naturally into four paragraphs of six verses each: vss. 1-6, 7-12, 13-18, and 19-24.

In vss. 1-6, the poet voices his deep gratitude in knowing that God understands him completely (no matter what man might think). True, God is "omniscient" (he knows all) in the abstract, but the psalmist's point is that God knows *him personally*. Four times in the paragraph (vss. 1, 2, 4, 6), as well as three other times in the psalm (vss. 14, 23 [twice]), he emphasizes that God "knows" him. This does not mean simply that God knows certain facts about him, but that he understands him and has an intimate personal relationship with him. God knows him because he has "searched" him (vss. 1, 3). Two different Hebrew words are translated "search" in these verses. The word in v. 1 means literally "to dig for precious metals" (it is so used in *Job* 28:3). The word in v. 3 means literally "to winnow," and thus conveys the thought that God had both thoroughly examined the author's heart and separated the good from the bad (the wheat from the chaff).

God knows all his daily habits ("all his ways," v. 3): such routine matters as sitting down, rising up (v. 2), travelling, and lying down (v. 3). He discerns his thoughts "from afar" (v. 2). The poet's thought is not that God is far from man, but still understands his thoughts. In a much more personal way, he means that God fully comprehends his thoughts while they are in the process of being formed in his mind. The Lord knows the background of his thinking, the human limitations which make his ideas less pure and polished than he would like for them to be. He knows not only what man actually thinks, but what in the very depths of his heart he would like to think. God reads and interprets his thoughts with a loving heart even before he thinks them.

"Even before" a word is on the psalmist's tongue, God knows it "altogether" (v. 4). He understands and sympathizes with all the parental strengths and weaknesses, all the influences of society, and all the personal experiences (good and bad) that lie behind and produce his words. He listens not only to what the poet says, but more intently to what he means, and more than this he is concerned about the full meaning of his words. Thus, the author is constantly aware that God completely surrounds him (v. 5). He confronts God at every turn of the road (see *Isaiah* 52:12). One is reminded of the encouraging words of *Psalm* 125:2:

> "As the mountains are round about Jerusalem,
> so the Lord is round about his people,
> from this time forth and for evermore."

In vss. 7-12, the psalmist rejoices in God's presence wherever he goes or even might go. Again, he does not speak abstractly of God's "omnipresence" (the idea that God is everywhere at all times), but of God's personal presence with him at every moment. If he were to travel at a slow deliberate gait ("go") or at the fastest speed imaginable ("flee"), he could not get away from God (v. 7). If he could go to the heights of the sky ("heaven") or to the depths of the grave ("Sheol"), God would be there. If he went to the farthest reaches of earth ("the uttermost parts of the sea," v. 9), he could not escape from God (vss. 9-10). If he tried to hide in the cover of deepest darkness, God would easily find him (vss. 11–12). The synonymous parallelism in v. 7 shows that God's "Spirit" means God's "presence," and thus "Spirit" here is not to be interpreted in the sense of the New Testament teaching of the "Holy Spirit," the third member of the Godhead. The "wings of the morning" (v. 9) have been variously understood, but it seems most natural to interpret them as the beams of light emanating from the sun as day dawns. In other words, the psalmist might travel as fast as light, but he still could not get away from God.

In vss. 13-18, the poet is struck with the care and thought that went into his own creation and personality. He was not "thrown together" as a kind of afterthought, but God "knit him together" in his mother's womb (v. 13) as an experienced artisan would weave a beautiful basket. He was "intricately wrought" "in secret," "in the depths of the earth" (v. 15). The Lord gave him his particular set of intellectual and emotional propensities (he "formed his inward parts," v. 13), and thus knows him better than anyone else could know him, even better than he knows himself (v. 14). And now, while others accuse him of wrong (v. 19), God judges him in light of the kind of person he made him to be. Before the psalmist's birth, God determined the best time to create him, and the length of his service on earth. And he wrote these in his heavenly book (v. 16), so that no schemes of men to destroy him could change the length of life that God intended for him to live.

The idea that God records a man's name and the length of his life in a heavenly book is quite familiar in the Old Testament (see e.g., *Exodus* 32:32-33; *Psalms* 56:8; 69:28; *Malachi* 3:16). It is difficult to see how God could "add fifteen years" to Hezekiah's life (*Isaiah* 38:5) unless he had predetermined how long Hezekiah would live in the first place. Also, both Old and New Testaments teach that God puts men on earth at certain times for specific works. God says to Jeremiah at the prophet's call:

> "Before I formed you in the womb I knew you,
>   and before you were born I consecrated you;
>   I appointed you a prophet to the nations." (*Jeremiah* 1:5).

And the apostle Paul declares that God had "set him apart before he was born" to preach the gospel to the Gentiles (*Galatians* 1:15-16; see also *Acts* 9:15). The lives and teachings of Jeremiah and Paul, as well as scriptures throughout the Bible, show that this does not mean that any man is not responsible for his thoughts, words, or actions. The length of a man's life does not determine the kind of man he is. God does not force a man to do what God puts him on earth to do. And that God *knows* what man will do does not mean that he *predetermines* or *forces* him to do it.

Some have been offended at the last paragraph (vss. 19-24), especially because of vss. 21-22, where the psalmist says that he "hates" God's enemies with a "perfect hatred," and have suggested that the offensive verses should be removed to another psalm or to other psalms. However, this feeling grows out of a narrow definition of hatred, or comes from a conviction that all hatred is sin. Biblically speaking at least, hatred does not necessarily carry with it the connotation of uncontrolled anger or of ill will. For example, Jesus says: "If any one comes to me and does not *hate* his own father and mother and wife and children and brothers and sisters, yes, and even his own life, he cannot be my disciple" (*Luke* 14:26). *Proverbs* 6:16-19 gives a list of seven things that God *hates*. Paul says that God *hated* Esau (*Romans* 9:13). The author of the book of Hebrews states that Christ *hated* lawlessness (*Hebrews* 1:9). Other examples could be given. But the point is that hatred, rightly defined and properly channeled, is an indispensable characteristic of God's servant. There is a real conflict between good and evil in the world. Exponents of evil are enemies of God. God cannot be neutral in this conflict. He is diametrically opposed to evil; he *hates* it completely. Thus, his genuine followers must hate it "with perfect (complete) hatred" (v. 22). Surely, God's child must love the sinner in the sense that his heart goes out to him and he yearns for his repentance and salvation. But at the same time he must hate him in the sense of staunchly withstanding him in the evil that he promotes.

It is significant that the psalmist does not voice his feelings against God's enemies in a vindictive or arrogant manner. Instead, he realizes that he must continually subject himself to God's careful scrutiny of his own heart, lest he too be or become a proponent of evil. Here we encounter the important prayer:

> "Search me, O God, and know my heart!
>   Try me and know my thoughts!
> And see if there be any wicked way in me,
>   and lead me in the way of everlasting!" (vss. 23-24).

REVIEW QUESTIONS

1. Describe the problems faced by the author of *Psalm* 7. Have you ever faced similar problems? Share your experiences with the class.

2. Give a three point outline of *Psalm* 7, then state in your own words the content of this psalm.

3. Read carefully *Psalm* 7:14 and *James* 1:14-15. What important lesson do these passages teach concerning the nature of sin and the relationship between temptation and sin? What practical lessons can be learned from this? Discuss.

4. List the four proofs that the author of *Psalm* 26 gives to prove his innocence. What important lesson does this teach about one's character and reputation? Discuss.

5. Read carefully *Psalms* 26:6; 73:13; *Deuteronomy* 21:6-7; and *Matthew* 27:24. What did "washing the hands" symbolize in biblical times? Discuss.

6. Discuss the kind of situation in which the author of *Psalm* 139 found himself. Have you ever encountered similar situations? Share your experiences with the class.

7. Read *Psalm* 139:1, 2, 4, 6, 14, 23. According to these verses, what is involved in the idea of God "knowing" man? Are there any practical lessons that modern man can learn from this? Discuss.

8. Study carefully *Psalm* 139:2, 4. Is it possible for a man to misunderstand or misinterpret the "thoughts" and "words" of his fellowman? Why is this? Does it give you personal encouragement to know that God knows what you really mean when you speak? Discuss at length the importance of the lesson intended here for Christian fellowship.

9. *Psalm* 139:7-12 teaches that there is no way for a man to escape from God. Does the psalmist think this is a good thing or a bad thing? What do you think? Discuss.

10. Read *Psalm* 139:13-16. Do you feel that God took special care in making you as you are? Do you believe he put you on earth at the ideal time? What kind of self-image do these truths give you? Discuss.

11. Does the Bible teach that God "hates"? See *Proverbs* 6:16-19; *Romans* 9:13. Does it teach that Christ "hates"? See *Hebrews* 1:9. Is it ever right for a Christian to hate? See *Luke* 14:26; *Psalm* 139:21-22. Discuss at length.

Lesson VIII

TO GOD ALONE BELONGS THE VICTORY

"Be strong and of good courage. do not be afraid or dismayed before the king of Assyria and all the horde that is with him; for there is one greater with us than with him. With him is an arm of flesh; but with us is the Lord our God, to help us and to fight our battles." (II Chronicles 32:7-8).

Man is constantly plagued with the temptation of thinking of himself more highly than he ought to think (*Romans* 12:3). He enjoys taking credit for what he views as his own accomplishments. Some boast of their financial successes, others of their military strength, and still others of their good works. All such boasting is vain in the eyes of God. Attention is now focused on three psalms in which God's people deny that their successes were due to their own abilities, and give credit for their good fortune to God alone.

Psalm 44

This psalm was composed shortly after an Israelite or Judean king and his army had been defeated by an enemy army. The enemy had taken spoil from God's people (v. 10), carried some of the Israelites into captivity (v. 11), and disgraced the king and his subjects before the nations (vss. 13-16). Scholars have suggested a number of historical events as the possible background for this psalm, including Sennacherib's invasion of Judah during the reign of Hezekiah (701 B. C.), Josiah's death at Megiddo at the hands of

Egyptian soldiers under Pharaoh-neco (609 B. C.), the aftermath of the rebellion of the western states (including Judah) against the Persian king Artaxerxes Ochus (351 B. C.), and the persecution of the Jews by the Seleucid (Syrian) king Antiochus IV Epiphanes (167 B. C.). The last date seems too late, because the book of Psalms seems already to have been completed by 200 B. C. or somewhat earlier. In light of the claim that God's people have been faithful to the covenant (vss. 17, 20), a setting shortly after Josiah's death is attractive. But the psalm gives such little specific information about the event that lay behind its composition that it is impossible to know for sure what it was.

The speakers in *Psalm* 44 alternate between the first person singular ("I," etc. vss. 4, 6, 15) and the first person plural ("we," etc., vss. 1, 5, 7, 8, 9, 10, 11, 13, 14, 17, 18, 19, 20, 22, 23, 24, 25). The individual is apparently the leader of the people; he may be a priest, but it is much more likely that he is the king, because of the strong military tone of the song. The psalm falls naturally into four parts. (1) The king and his people declare that just as God had delivered their fathers from their enemies, he had also delivered them from their enemies (vss. 1-8). (2) But in a recent battle or war, God had not gone out with his armies, and thus Israel had been severely defeated (vss. 9-16). (3) There is no logical explanation for this defeat, as Israel had been faithful to the covenant of the Lord (vss. 17-22). (4) The worshippers beg God to intervene and deliver them from their enemies, as he had done before (vss. 23-26).

In vss. 1-8, the king of Israel denies that he is really the king of God's people, and affirms that God is (v. 4). He denies that Israel was ever victorious by her own strength, and proclaims that God always gave Israel the victory. Previous generations passed down to the present generation accounts of God's intervention in behalf of his people. This information was communicated *orally*—"our fathers have *told* us"; "we have *heard*" (v. 1). Specifically, the psalmist tells how *God* drove out the nations before Israel during the conquest of Canaan, and settled Israel in her new land (v. 2),

"for not by their own sword did they win the land,
   nor did their own arm give them victory;
   but thy right hand, and thy arm,
   and the light of thy countenance" (v. 3).

The present generation has also experienced God's saving power. They know they are victorious only because they trust in God (vss. 5, 7). The king declares:

"Not in my bow do I trust,
   nor can my sword save me" (v. 7).

In vss. 9-16, the king and his people bemoan their recent loss to some enemy army. They are convinced that the reason they lost is that God did not go forth with his armies (v. 9). They picture God as a merchant who sold Israel to her foes at a very cheap price (v. 12). They followed him confidently as sheep follow a shepherd, but he had led them to slaughter before their enemies (v. 11; see also v. 22). This figure of sheep being led to a slaughter is used frequently in scripture of innocent, trusting people who follow a course of life that is destined to lead to their destruction. When Jeremiah learned that his friends from his home town in Anathoth were plotting to destroy him while pretending to be his close companion, he cried:

"I was like a gentle lamb
   led to the slaughter" (*Jeremiah* 11:19).

Isaiah 53:7 describes the "suffering servant" of the Lord in this way:

"Like a lamb that is led to the slaughter,
   and like a sheep that before its shearers is dumb,
so he opened not his mouth."

It was this scripture that the Ethiopian eunuch was reading when Philip intercepted him on the road from Jerusalem to Gaza, and with which Philip began as he preached Jesus unto him. (*Acts* 8:32-35). And Paul quotes *Psalm* 44:22 and applies it to Christians in his powerful description of the role that they must play in the world (*Romans* 8:36).

In vss. 17-22, God's people voice their amazement at the humiliation which the Lord has brought upon them. God "knows the secrets of the heart" (v. 21); he knows whether they are true to him as they claim to be. And they affirm that their "heart" has not turned against him (v. 18). They have been "true" to the "covenant," not "false" (v. 17). In other words, they have maintained an intimate personal relationship with him, and have refused to worship ("spread forth their hands to") "a strange god" (v. 20).

In light of this, in the final paragraph (vss. 23-26), they ask God "why" he has not intervened in their behalf (v. 24). They are "afflicted," "oppressed" (v. 24), and "bowed down" (v. 25). Is there any logical reason why God has overthrown his people at the hand of their enemies? Absolutely not! Therefore, they appeal to God to "wake up" (v. 23), get out of bed ("rise up"), and come to "deliver" them from their terrible plight (v. 26).

Psalm 124

This psalm was composed shortly after Israel had been delivered from a powerful enemy. There is not enough information in the psalm to allow us to determine the exact historical event lying behind it. It falls naturally into two parts. (1) A priest calls on Israel to reflect on what the outcome of the battle would have been if God had not been on her side (vss. 1-5). Some scholars think the priest's words terminate at v. 1, but it seems more likely that he continues speaking through v. 5. (2) The people respond by praising God for helping them in time of deep distress (vss. 6-8).

Four figures are used in this song to describe the great might of the enemy that God had overcome. They were like: (a) a great monster that would have swallowed Israel up alive (v. 3); (b) a raging flood that would have swept them away (vss. 4-5); (c) a hungry lion that would have seized them as prey (v. 6); and (d) a fowler's snare that would have trapped them like a bird caught in a net (v. 7).

This song gives three insights into the role the Lord plays in such a situation of conflict. First, he is "on the side of" his people (vss. 1, 2), assuming that they are faithful to him. It is he who fights their battles. Second, he has such control over his people (and for that matter over all mankind) that he can "give" them into the hands of their enemies (v. 6). Indeed, on a number of occasions he has given them over to their enemies to punish them or to carry out his purposes, but in this instance he did not, and his people are grateful. Third, he who helps his people "made heaven and earth" (v. 8; see *Genesis* 14:19, 22). As creator of all that is, God has control over all that is, and can use individuals and nations to carry out his purposes. How comforting it is for God's people to know that their helper is the all-powerful creator of the universe! The "name" of the Lord (v. 8) means the Lord himself or his saving presence.

Psalm 121

There is no agreement among scholars as to the kind of situation in which this psalm was produced. (a) Some think a worshipper is talking to himself, and thus "you" and "your" (which is second person singular in Hebrew) in vss. 3-8 simply represent one way a person can address himself. (b) Others think that the "hills" in v. 1 are the mountains on which the city of Jerusalem rests, and that this psalm is a dialogue between two worshippers as they go on their way to Jerusalem to worship God at a great festival. The psalmist speaks in vss. 1-2, and his fellow traveller replies in vss. 3-8 with words of encouragement. (c) It seems best to take the "hills" in v. 1 to be the mountains around Jerusalem on which the Canaanites, and the Israelites themelves, built "high places" (see the reflection of Israel's apostasy in adopting the worship on the high places [the Hebrew word for "high place" is *bamah*] in *Ezekiel* 20:28-31). The worshipper has just attended a festival at Jerusalem to worship the true God. As he prepares to leave and contemplates the perils of the road that all travellers faced in ancient time (recall the story of the Good Samaritan, *Luke* 10:30-37), he yearns for assurance that he will make it home safely. He lifts up his eyes to the "hills," where many Israelites worship the Canaanite Baals, as if to ask himself whether they could or would protect him on his journey. But no sooner does the thought cross his mind than he replies:

"My help comes from the Lord,
who made heaven and earth." (v. 2).

The similarity with *Psalm* 124:8 is immediately apparent. The poet will put his trust in the creator of all that is, and not in idols made by the hands of men.

In vss. 3-8, apparently a temple priest buttresses his decision by declaring that God, the "keeper" of Israel (v. 4), can and will also "keep" him. Since some form of the verb "keep" occurs six times in this tiny psalm (vss. 3, 4, 5, 7 [twice], 8), this is surely the theme that holds it together.

The assurances that the priest gives the psalmist are most appropriate for a man about to set out on a journey. He declares that God: (a) will not allow disaster to strike him on the road (vss. 3a, 7a); (b) will not sleep, but will protect him, while the psalmist takes his rest (vss. 3b-4); (c) will protect him from sunstroke and "moonstroke" (vss. 5-6); (d) will keep him alive during his journey (v. 7b); and (e) will guard him as he leaves the temple or the city of Jerusalem ("your going out"), and as he enters his own city or his own home ("your coming in") (v. 8). As a matter of fact, the Lord will keep him "from this time forth and for evermore" (v. 8). It is quite obvious that "for evermore" here does not mean "eternity," but rather as long as the psalmist lives.

REVIEW QUESTIONS

1. Describe the historical setting presupposed in *Psalm* 44. Name some events in Israel's history that could fit the description given here. Which do you think is the most likely? Give good arguments to support your view.

2. Give a four point outline of *Psalm* 44, then state in your own words the content of this psalm.

3. Study carefully *Psalm* 44:3, 7. What important lesson do these verses teach? What practical lesson can the Christian learn from this? Discuss.

4. Read *Psalm* 44:11, 22. Use a concordance and find as many passages as you can which speak of people being led as sheep to the slaughter. What does this expression mean? How does the author of *Psalm* 44 use it? How is it used in other biblical texts? Discuss in particular the way Paul uses *Psalm* 44:22 in *Romans* 8:36.

5. What four figures are used in *Psalm* 124 to describe the mighty power of the enemy that had recently attacked Israel? What is the author of this psalm trying to emphasize by using these figures? Discuss.

6. According to *Psalm* 124:1, 2, 6, 8, what three roles does the Lord play in situations of conflict? Give your own personal experiences in which you see the Lord working in one or more of these ways. Share your thoughts with the class.

7. Discuss the different views on the kind of setting lying behind *Psalm* 121. Which do you think is the most likely? Why?

8. What is the theme of *Psalm* 121? Give good arguments for your answer.

9. List the five assurances that the temple priest gives the poet in *Psalm* 121:3-8. What kind of situation do such assurances fit most appropriately?

Lesson IX

GOD'S ETERNITY AND MAN'S TRANSITORINESS

"My days are swifter than a weaver's shuttle" (Job 7:6).

All men are faced with the reality of death and of the brevity of life. Whereas many would attempt various means of avoiding a forthright confrontation of such sobering realities, it is to the credit of inspired speakers and writers of the Bible that they meet these crises head-on. Some of the most familiar passages of scripture deal with this problem.

> "All flesh is like grass
> and all its glory like the flower of grass.
> The grass withers, and the flower falls,
> but the word of the Lord abides for ever." (*I Peter* 1:24-25).
>
> "For I am already on the point of being sacrificed; the time of my departure has come. I have fought the good fight, I have finished the race, I have kept the faith." (*II Timothy* 4:6-7).
>
> "I am about to go the way of all the earth. Be strong and show yourself a man" (*I Kings* 2:2).
>
> "For to me to live is Christ, and to die is gain" (*Philippians* 1:21).
>
> "It is appointed for men to die once, and after that comes judgement" (*Hebrews* 9:27).

This lesson treats two beautiful psalms that emphasize man's transitoriness, and contrast this with God's eternal nature.

Psalm 102

This psalm was composed by a Jew living in Babylonian exile (between 587 and 536 B.C.). Zion is in ruins with the stones of its temple and walls lying in the dust (vss. 13-14), and thus needs to be rebuilt (v. 16). In Babylon, the poet and his comrades are in prison and apparently have been sentenced to death (v. 20). They are destitute and helpless (v. 17). The poet is in the prime of life (vss. 23-24), but (possibly because of lack of food and bad treatment in prison at the hands of the Babylonians) is very sick and near death. He is running a high fever ("my bones burn like a furnace," v. 3), he has no appetite (vss. 4, 9), he is steadily losing weight (vss. 5-6), and he cannot sleep (v. 7). To make matters worse, his enemies taunt him all the time (v. 8), and he is convinced that his misfortunes are due directly to God's anger (vss. 10, 23-24), which may indicate that he is acknowledging that the destruction of Zion was God's punishment on the Jews for their many sins, and that his own afflictions are God's punishment for his sins.

Psalm 102 may be divided into two parts (vss. 1-17 and 18-28), each containing an appeal for God to intervene in behalf of the poet and his companions (vss. 1-2 and 18—22), a description of the psalmist's pitiable condition (vss. 3-11 and 23-24), and an assurance that the eternal God will save his people from their terrible misfortunes (vss. 12-17, 25-28). It is most significant that the author's own destitute condition has made him keenly aware of the transitory nature of his own life, the eternal nature of God, his participation in God's chosen people, and the responsibility he has to the coming generation.

In vss. 1-2 and 18-22, the psalmist pleads with God to hear his prayer and deliver him and his fellows from their distress. It seems likely that in vss. 1-2 he has simply combined several expressions of appeal to God that were common in temple worship, as a comparison of these expressions with other appeals in the Psalms might indicate (see e.g., *Psalms* 27:9; 39:12; 69:17; 143:7). In vss. 18-22, the poet gives two reasons why God should "look down from heaven at the earth" (v. 19), "hear the groans of the prisoners," and "set free those who were doomed to die" (v. 20). (1) The coming generation will be able to look back on such a mighty deed of God and praise his name in Jerusalem (vss. 18, 21). (2) Other nations will learn what God has done for his suffering people. This will show them that the Lord is compassionate in his nature. They will thus be attracted to him, gather to Jerusalem, and worship him (v. 22).

In vss. 3-11 and 23-24, the author describes his own destitute condition. He gives a vivid description of his illness, accompanied by fever (v. 3), loss of appetite (vss. 4, 9), declining weight (vss. 5-6), and inability to sleep (v. 7). All this brings home to him a fundamental reality of life, viz., that one's physical existence on earth is uncertain and at best very brief. But he is in the prime of life (he is "in the midst of his days," v. 24); God has "shortened his days" (v. 23), for he is near death. Here the psalmist uses three graphic figures to depict the brevity of life. He says it is like: (a) smoke billowing from a chimney that quickly passes away (v. 3); (b) an evening shadow that lengthens out across the land; and (c) grass that withers away under the heat of the sun (v. 11). His distress is intensified by the continual taunts of his enemies (v. 8), and the certainty that God is punishing him for his sins (v. 10).

But in spite of all these severe problems, in vss. 12-17 and 25-28 the author proclaims his confidence that God will raise up his afflicted people and bless their descendants. His confidence is based on two deep convictions. First, he firmly believes that God will answer the prayers of his suffering people (v. 17). And second, if God restores his exiled people to Jerusalem and causes them to restore the temple and the walls that the Babylonians have destroyed, the nations will be converted to him (v. 15).

Throughout this psalm, the poet is struck with the striking contrast between his own transitoriness and God's eternity. He declares that God is enthroned (sits as king) for ever, and that his name endures to all generations (v. 24). There never was when God was not, for he created the heavens and the earth (v. 25), and thus must have existed before they came into existence. Likewise, there never will be when God will not be. His years have no end (v. 27). The heavens and the earth which he created will perish and wear out like a garment, and then God will exchange them for other clothing, as it were (v. 26), but God will continue to exist on and on (v. 27), and thus the next generation will be secure under his care (v. 28). It is worthy of note that vss. 25-27 are quoted in *Hebrews* 1:10-12 and applied to Christ, apparently in a typological sense.

Psalm 90

Because of the use of the first person plural ("we," "our," "us") throughout this psalm (vss. 1, 7, 8, 9, 10, 12, 14, 15, 17), many scholars conclude that it was composed *by* a group of Israelites and with *their concerns* in mind. This is supported by the mention of "*thy* (i.e., God's) servants" in vss. 13 and 16. However, the whole tenor of the song seems to suggest that it was composed by an individual Jew who felt very strong affinities with all mankind. In this case, the first person plural should be equated with "man" (meaning mankind) and "children of men" in v. 3, and with "men" in v. 5. Possibly the intended emphasis in vss. 13 and 16 is on "servants" (man, by his very position as a created being, is a servant of God, and not one who can dictate to or control him), rather than on the possessive pronoun "thy." The content of this psalm does not allow it to be connected with any kind of concrete situation. The heading connects it with "Moses, the man of God," but there is no way to determine whether the headings of the psalms were authentic and inspired (see Volume I, Lesson III).

Psalm 90 falls naturally into two parts. (1) The poet vividly contrasts the eternal nature of God with the transitory nature of man (vss. 1-12). (2) He pleads with God to be compassionate with sinful, suffering man, and to bless his work that he might feel that he has been of some value on earth (vss. 13-17).

In vss. 1-12, the psalmist begins by affirming that God is eternal. And he applies this both to the past, and to the future in this psalm. There never was when God was not. He has been man's dwelling place as long as man has lived on earth ("in all generations," v. 1); in other words, man has always depended on God (whether he was aware of it or not) for food, shelter, clothing, and even life itself. But even beyond this, before the primeval waters of chaos receded and the mountains appeared, yea, before the earth was created, God was (v. 2). But looking to the future, there never will be when God will not be. He who was "*from* everlasting" is also "*to* everlasting" (v. 2). Not only does he work in a man's life today, but he will also be present to help him as long as he lives (and so the poet looks forward to God's help in the future of his own life, vss. 12, 14-17); and then when he is gone, he will be present to help his children and his grandchildren, etc. (v. 16).

In contrast to this, man is transient. God turns him back to the dust whence he came (v. 3; see   *Genesis* 2:7; 3:19), "consumes" him, "overwhelms" him (v. 7), and he is "soon gone" (v. 10). The psalmist uses six figures to describe the brevity of man's life. It is like: (a) yesterday when it is past (v. 4); (b) a watch in the night (v. 4; the Jews divided the night into three watches of four hours each, while the Greeks and Romans divided it into four watches of three hours each; *Mark* 13:35 designates the four watches being used in New Testament times as "evening," "midnight," "cockcrow," and "morning"; see also *Mark* 6:48); (c) a dream (v. 5); (d) grass that flourishes in the morning, but under the hot sun fades and withers by evening (vss. 5-6); (e) a sigh (v. 9); and (f) swift flight (v. 10). The poet's thoughts are briefly summed up in the familiar words of verse 10:

> "The years of our life are threescore and ten,
>   or even by reason of strength fourscore;
> yet their span is but toil and trouble;
>   they are soon gone, and we fly away."

But the author emphasizes that there is a reason for the brevity of man's life, and for the suffering that he experiences in that brief span (see vss. 10, 15). It is that man is filled with sin, both sins of which he is aware and sins of which he is not aware ("secret sins," see *Psalm* 19:12; *Ecclesiastes* 12:14); and God in his "anger" and "wrath" punishes men with death for their iniquities (vss. 7, 9, 11). The principle that sin brings death is emphasized from the very beginning of the Bible (see *Genesis* 2:16-17; 3:1-4, 17-19).

But earthly life is as much a reality as death. Thus, the psalmist prays that God might help man live his brief life on earth to the fullest. First, he asks God to "teach man to number his days that he might get a heart of wisdom" (v. 12). In other words, he begs God to help man realize how brief his life is on earth, in order that he might use his time in the most meaningful way possible, which is to learn "wisdom." In Old Testament thought, wisdom is not a great volume of facts (although correct facts are helpful in attaining true wisdom), but "fearing the Lord" (see *Proverbs* 1:7; 9:10; *Psalm* 111:10; *Job* 28:28). However, to "fear" the Lord is not to be terrified by him, but to hold him in the highest respect, to reverence him, to honor him, to put him first in every aspect of life (see *Psalms* 22:23; 33:8; *Malachi* 1:6). Second, he asks the Lord to help man joyfully accept the limitations and sufferings of life (vss. 14-15). It is significant that he does not ask for escape from life's problems, but rather the faith to live with them joyfully and hopefully. Third, he prays that God will guide the present generation to do something useful in order that their work might not be in vain, and in order that the coming generation might benefit from it (vss. 16-17). In this way, the workers may perish, but their work will continue.

REVIEW QUESTIONS

1. Study carefully *I Peter* 1:24-25; *II Timothy* 4:6-7; *I Kings* 2:2; *Philippians* 1:21; *Hebrews* 9:27. What does each of these passages teach about the brevity of life and the certainty of death? What practical lessons can the Christian learn from this? Discuss.

2. Describe the historical setting lying behind *Psalm* 102. Have you ever suffered similar afflictions? Share your experiences with the class.

3. Give a two point outline of *Psalm* 102. Show the connection between each of the three subdivisions of the first part and each of the three subdivisions of the second part. Tell in your own words the content of this psalm.

4. What three figures does the author of *Psalm* 102 use to show the brevity of life? See vss. 3 and 11. How meaningful are these figures to you? Discuss.

5. Discuss the eternal nature of God as it is depicted in *Psalm* 102:12, 24-28. What lessons can man learn from this truth?

6. What are two ways that the first person plural ("we," etc.) of *Psalm* 90 can be interpreted? Which do you think is correct? Why? Study a number of commentaries on this problem, and share what you learn with the class.

7. Give a two point outline of *Psalm* 90, then tell in your own words the content of this psalm.

8. Discuss the eternal nature of God as it is pictured in *Psalm* 90:1-2, 12, 14-17. What practical lessons can the Christian learn from this?

9. List the six figures used by the author of *Psalm* 90 to depict the brevity of life. See vss. 4-6, 9-10. Are these figures meaningful to you? Discuss.

10. In what three ways does the author of *Psalm* 90 ask God to help man live a meaningful life on earth? See vss. 12, 14-17. Discuss the importance of these concepts in living your own life for the Lord.

Lesson X

THE DECEITFULNESS OF RICHES

"But those who desire to be rich fall into temptation, into a snare, into many senseless and hurtful desires that plunge men into ruin and destruction. For the love of money is the root of all evils." (I Timothy 6:9-10).

It is an undeniable fact of life that man has always been enamored by wealth. He tends to have an insatiable desire for possessions and money. The gaining of riches is the major goal of many a life. And God's people are not exempt from this craze for wealth. Inspired speakers and writers had to address themselves to this problem many times, and their outlooks on the role of possessions in the righteous man's life are always relevant to the struggles of the growing Christian. Several psalms deal with this problem. This lesson calls attention to two of these.

Psalm 37

This psalm is an acrostic in which every other line begins with the next succeeding letter in the Hebrew alpabet. Usually this means that every other verse begins with a new letter, but there are three exceptions to this, vss. 8, 20, 28b. The author is an old man (vss. 25, 35-36), who is trying to teach a younger man (in Hebrew, the second person pronouns "you," "your," etc., are singular throughout the psalm) the importance of trusting in God in a time when it appears that the wicked are succeeding and the righteous are failing. At the time the poet composed this psalm, wicked men controlled (possessed) the land (the text does not make it clear whether this means the entire land of Canaan, or

North Israel, or South Judah, or something else) (vss. 1, 7, 9, 10, 16, 20, 28, 34-36, 38). It is possible, of course, that the wicked in this psalm are foreigners who have invaded Israel and taken possession of the land, but the psalm gives the impression that what is at stake is the family inheritance that was handed down from generation to generation among the Jews. The wicked appear to be rich Jews who are engaged in endless land grabbing, and will stop at nothing to get what they want. Thus, the poor suffer in a variety of ways, not the least of which is that their property is taken from them by force, much like Ahab seized the vineyard of Naboth (see *I Kings* 21) (vss. 7, 12, 14, 25, 32-33, 40). Unfortunately, such practices were common in ancient Israel (see e.g., *Amos* 2:6-8; 8:4-6; *Isaiah* 5:8-10; *Micah* 2:1-2, 8-9; *Jeremiah* 7:5-7). This psalm could have been composed almost any time during the period of the monarchy. Its thought and structure are much like the wisdom sayings in Job, Proverbs, and Ecclesiastes, and it was probably authored by one of the "wise men" (see *Jeremiah* 18:18; *Proverbs* 22:17; 24:23).

The acrostic form and the repetition of ideas and phrases throughout *Psalm* 37 make it very difficult to give a convincing meaningful outline. With hesitation, we suggest that it may be divided into four parts. (1) The old psalmist advises his young student to trust in the Lord to right the wrongs that seem to exist in the world rather than to constantly bemoan the apparent prosperity of the wicked and poverty of the righteous (vss. 1-11). (2) He declares that God will cut off the wicked in his own good time and in his own way (vss. 12-20). (3) He confidently affirms that the righteous will survive and succeed, in spite of the way things look at the present time (vss. 21-31). (4) He contrasts the ultimate success of the righteous and failure of the wicked (vss. 32-40).

In vss. 1-11, the author boldly confronts the temptation of the righteous man to "envy" the wicked man's apparent success (v. 1). Such a feeling can cause the servant of God to think that the way to prosperity is to be gained through "evil devices" (v. 7). The relevance of this point is verified by many examples of godly people who have turned their backs on the Lord because it did not appear that he was blessing their lives with those things that the wicked around them were receiving. Three times in this paragraph, the poet warns: "Fret not yourself" because of the wicked man's prosperity (vss. 1, 7, 8). Instead, "trust in the Lord" (vss. 3, 5), "take delight in him" (v. 4), "commit your way to him" (v. 5), control your feelings of anger against seeming injustices in the world (v. 8), and "wait patiently for the Lord to act" (vss. 7, 9). And he gives the young man two reasons why he should trust in the Lord and not envy the wicked man's success. (1) The wicked man's prosperity will not last. It will "soon" (in a "little while") fade like the grass and wither like the green herb (vss. 2, 9-10). (2) In good time, those who trust in God will "possess the land." This theme is very prominent throughout the psalm (vss. 3, 9, 11, 22, 29, 34). The thought is that although the inherited property that rightfully belongs to various poor people in Israel that are trying to live for God is in the hands of the wicked rich, in God's own time it will be wrested from the rich and returned to the poor. Jesus uses the Hebrew word translated "land" in v. 11 in the sense of "earth" (globe, planet), and promises that the meek shall inherit the earth (apparently in a spiritual sense, *Matthew* 5:5).

In vss. 12-20, the psalmist declares unhesitatingly that the wicked cannot prevail. There is something in the very nature of sin that corrupts and destroys (v. 13). Unlike the righteous, the wicked do not have that inner quality of life and stability that enables them to stand in "evil times" and in "days of famine" (v. 19). Like grass in the field and smoke billowing from a chimney, they vanish away (v. 20). Furthermore, they are self-centered, and feel no compassion for the underprivileged. On the contrary, they lay wicked plots against the righteous (v. 12), and seek to destroy the poor and needy (v. 14). Thus, their doom is sealed!

In vss. 21-31, the poet affirms just as confidently that the righteous will ultimately succeed. This is based on four arguments. (1) The righteous trusts in God under all circumstances, and not in his own ability or righteousness (vss. 24, 31). (2) He shows genuine compassion to those that are in

need, and strives to see justice prevail (vss. 27-28, 30). (3)
When he is blessed with wealth, he does not horde it to
himself, but gives liberally to those that are destitute (vss. 21,
26). (4) Experiences of a long life show that, though times
may be hard, the righteous is never deprived of the necessities
of life. Here we encounter a familiar text:

> "I have been young, and now am old;
>   yet I have not seen the righteous forsaken
>   or his children begging bread." (v. 25).

In vss. 32-40, the author declares that in the end the
wicked will be cut off, and the righteous will prevail. A
wicked man constantly looks for opportunities to bring the
righteous to court in order to obtain a verdict against him
that will destroy him financially or socially, or even lead to
his death (vss. 32-33). But God will not allow the wicked to
succeed in such ungodly endeavors (vss. 33, 35-36, 38, 40).
Rather, he will defend the righteous (vss. 37, 39-40), and the
day will come when the righteous will see his enemy fall (v.
34), and then he will know from his own experience that
human life is in the hands of a just God.

Psalm 49

This psalm is indeed one of the jewels of the Psalter. Its
subject and the author's approach indicate that it was composed by one of the "wise men" (he professes to speak
"wisdom," vs. 3), skilled in composing proverbs to the
accompaniment of a lyre (v. 4), who knew what it was to be
persecuted by rich self-seekers, for the purpose of instructing
men concerning the futility of trusting in wealth. This theme
is clearly emphasized by the recurring refrain or chorus that
appears at the end of the two major sections of the psalm
(vss. 12, 20):

> "Man cannot abide in his pomp,
>   he is like the beasts that perish."

This song falls naturally into three parts: an introduction
(vss. 1-4); and two paragraphs (vss. 5-12 and 13-20), each

emphasizing that the wealthy will certainly die, and then their riches will be useless to them.

In the introduction (vss. 1-4), the poet is not satisfied to summon the Jews only to listen to his teaching. His subject is too universal, too common to all mankind, for that. And so he urges "all peoples," "all inhabitants of the world" (v. 1), "low and high," "rich and poor" (v. 2), to hear what he has to say. He has inclined his ear to a proverb (v. 4), which probably means that he himself has been instructed by divine inspiration on his subject. He has meditated on what he has learned (v. 3), and thus he is certain that what he has to say is "wisdom" (v. 3), and will be of utmost value to anyone who takes it seriously and lives by it.

In vss. 5-12, the author says that is is foolish to be afraid of what a rich man might do to him, or for that matter to anyone who is righteous or poor (v. 5; see also v. 16). The wealthy man may be able to buy himself out of many difficult problems in this life, but he cannot pay Death enough to keep from dying and to "continue to live on for ever" (vss. 7-9). All men must die and "leave their wealth to others" (v. 10). At death, the richest man becomes poor in this world's goods, even though the possessions he amassed still bear his name (v. 11).

In vss. 13-20, the psalmist emphasizes that material wealth is not a basic essential to man's existence, because man is immediately separated from his riches when he dies. Death is like a shepherd that leads all men like sheep into their eternal home in the grave (v. 14; see also vss. 11, 19). Therefore, it is senseless to be afraid of the power of a rich man (v. 16), because when he dies he "cannot take it with him" V. 17—"when he dies he will carry nothing away").

Verse 15 is the pivotal verse in this psalm, and of great importance in Old Testament thought. The poet says:

> "But God will ransom my soul from the power of Sheol,
> for he will receive me."

Scholars have interpreted these two lines in at least four different ways. (1) Some argue that it did not originally belong to this psalm, but was added by a later hand. However, there is no textual justification or contextual justification for such a position. And even if it were true, these lines would have been added long before Christian times. (2) Others believe it means that while the wicked rich can expect sudden and severe destruction, God will protect the righteous from such extreme adversity. (3) Similarly, others think that when the psalmist said this he was facing premature death or was being threatened with death, and thus was expressing his faith that God would deliver him from this immediate problem. Now, it is true that these two views agree with the statement in v. 10 that, not only the "foolish" and the "stupid," but also the "wise" die. But it is hard to see how the poet could feel that he was any better off than the wicked if eventually he would be consigned to the grave just like they are.

(4) Thus, several scholars believe that the author means that after he dies and goes to Sheol (the grave), God will raise him up and he will enjoy eternal communion with his maker. The following considerations seem to support this view. (a) Verse 15 is not only a contrast to v. 14, but also to v. 8, as the use of the word "ransom" in both verses shows. His thought is that while the rich cannot give God enough money to bribe him to ransom them from death (vss. 7-8), God will ransom the righteous from death by his own power (v. 15). (b) In v. 10, the psalmist recognizes that death is the great leveller of all men ("wise and "foolish" alike), and thus he also will die. But when he dies, something else will happen— God will receive him to himself. (c) If v. 15 refers only to divine deliverances in this life, really the psalmist is no better off than the wicked rich, because, like them, he will die and descend to the grave. (d) The word "receive" is the same word in Hebrew that is used of Enoch ("God *took* him," *Genesis* 5:24) and Elijah ("the Lord was about to *take* Elijah up to heaven," *II Kings* 2:1; see also vss. 3, 5, 9, 10) being caught up into heaven to be with God.

The term "for ever" occurs four times in *Psalm* 37 (vss.

18, 27, 28, 29) and twice in *Psalm* 49 (vss. 9, 11). All the instances in *Psalm* 37 pertain to man's life on this earth, and therefore in this psalm the expression must mean "for a long time," "for an indefinite period," or the like. However, in *Psalm* 49 it seems to mean "endless time." In v. 9 the concept is that if the rich man could, he would pay God a ransom so that he could live on this earth "for ever." And in v. 11, the poet apparently means that when the rich die they stay in the grave eternally ("for ever"), in contrast to which he looks for the time that God will "receive" him to himself (v. 15).

REVIEW QUESTIONS

1. What does the content of *Psalm* 37 indicate about its author, the circumstances lying behind it, and the author's purpose in composing it?

2. Give a four point outline of *Psalm* 37, then state in your own words the content of this psalm.

3. Read carefully *Psalm* 37:1, 7. Are you tempted to envy wealthy people? Do you know other Christians that have the same temptation? Discuss this problem frankly.

4. According to the author of *Psalm* 37, what is the best reaction to the temptation to envy wealthy men? See especially vss. 3-5, 7-9. Discuss the validity of this approach to the problem of envy.

5. What four arguments does the author of *Psalm* 37 make to support his confidence that ultimately the righteous will succeed? Verses 21-31. Discuss the validity of each of these arguments.

6. Study carefully *Psalm* 49:12, 20. In light of these two verses, what is the theme of *Psalm* 49?

7. Give a three point outline of *Psalm* 49, then tell in your own words the content of this psalm.

8. According to *Psalm* 49, why is it illogical for a servant of God to be afraid of what the rich might do to him? Discuss the significance of this for the thinking of a Christian?

9. Study *Psalm* 49:15 very carefully. Read several good commentaries on this verse. List at least four interpretations of the meaning of this passage. Which do you think is correct? Give good arguments to support your position. Do you think this passage teaches life after death? Does the Old Testament teach life after death? Discuss.

Lesson XI

GOD-CENTERED LIVING (I)

"The Lord is my shepherd, I shall not want." (Psalm 23:1).

Life at best is very short. Therefore, man needs to find the focal point that will make his life most meaningful and useful. People have sought this focal point in a variety of places, such as military power, social prestige, financial security, or personal righteousness. Ultimately all of these bring one short of man's greatest potential. Inspired biblical speakers and writers have blessed human life most of all by emphasizing the most significant focal point imaginable, viz., God-centered living. The next two lessons are devoted to analyzing certain psalms that bring out this point.

Psalm 73

The author of this psalm (the thought of which is similar to that found in *Psalms* 37 and 49) has passed through a very significant personal experience, in which his faith was deeply shaken by the apparent facts of life that were taking place around him, but then greatly strengthened by a personal communion with God in the Jerusalem temple ("sanctuary," v. 17). He feels that his experience was so important that he must share it with others who are having or may have a similar experience. This psalm demonstrates in a magnificent way that doubt may be an avenue that God uses to force the naive believer to rethink his faith and deepen his commitment to God.

Psalm 73 seems to fall naturally into two parts. (1) The poet relates the doubts that flooded his mind as he reflected on his own afflictions and the blessings of the wicked (vss. 1-14). (2) He tells how he came to see these matters in a new perspective when he went to the temple and communed with God (vss. 15-28).

In vss. 1-14, the psalmist begins by arresting the attention of his hearers with the conclusion to which his experience had led him:

"Truly God is good to the upright,
    to those who are pure in heart" (v. 1).

Observation of what life appears to be had "almost" and "well nigh" (v. 2) caused him to lose faith in God's "goodness." He had worked very hard to keep his heart clean, and had symbolically washed his hands in the temple worship to declare his innocence of sins (see *Deuteronomy* 21:6-7; *Psalm* 26:6; *Matthew* 27:24). But this seemed to be "all in vain" (v. 13), because he was stricken with a severe illness (v. 14).

His own distresses sharply contrasted with the apparent blessings of the wicked. They have good health (v. 4), are virtually free from trouble (v. 5), grown richer and richer (vss. 7, 12), do not hesitate to boast loud and long about their position among men and their successes (vss. 6, 8-9), and enjoy the respect and good will of God's people (vss. 10-11). Their wealth is gained through oppressing the poor and unfortunate (vss. 6, "violence," 8, "malice," "oppression"), and yet the people are so fearful of their power and desirous to share their prosperity by gaining their good will that they live according to the belief that God will do nothing to end this oppression or to punish these proud evildoers. They say:

"How can God know?
    Is there knowledge in the Most High?" (v. 11).

Of course, they do not deny the existence of God, but for all practical purposes their belief is atheistic, for since he does nothing in his world, it is the same as if he did not exist at all. This success story of the wicked around him had aroused the poet's envy. He was tempted to become arrogant, and to gain prosperity through wickedness (v. 3).

Then in vss. 15-28, the psalmist tells how he gained new insight into the true nature of life. Throughout his struggle with doubt, he had succeeded in keeping his thoughts to himself. Voicing his feelings would not have made the problem go away, and it might have hurt less mature members of God's people (v. 15). Instead, the author faced the issue squarely where it counted most—in the deepest recesses of his own mind and heart. The inner conflict was bitter for a while, "until" he brought his case before God in the temple (vss. 16-17). Up until this time, his attention had been riveted on the present situation. But now his mind is lifted above this to the "end," the final outcome of the wicked and the righteous (v. 17). And it dawns on him that sometimes things are not really what they appear to be. The truth is that the wicked are in a very precarious situation. They are like a man walking on slippery ground (v. 18). Their future is uncertain, they may be destroyed "in a moment" (v. 19). Their good fortune will seem like a "dream" when it suddenly comes to an end (v. 20).

Having reflected on his hidden desire to be like the wicked rich and on what he had come to see in the temple, the poet repents of his unbelief. He confesses:

"I was stupid and ignorant,
   I was like a beast toward thee." (v. 22)

And yet his doubt had caused him to renew his faith in God at a much deeper level than he had ever known before. It has made him realize that even when man forsakes God, God does not forsake him (vss. 23-24), and that there is nothing on earth so precious or valuable that it can take the place of daily communion with God. The psalmist declares:

"Whom have I in heaven but thee?
   And there is nothing upon earth that I desire besides
   thee." (v. 25)

Man's ultimate good is to be "near God," and out of this intimate personal relationship to tell of all his wonderful works (v. 28).

The last line of v. 24 plays a very important role in the thought of this psalm:

"Afterward thou wilt receive me to glory."

Some scholars think that this refers to divine deliverance and blessing in this life. However, this interpretation does not really make good sense in the context of this psalm, and therefore it seems best to agree with many other scholars who think that the poet means that even death itself cannot sever the beautiful communion that exists between God and his faithful people. Several arguments support this view. (1) The word "afterward" here most naturally is to be seen as parallel in meaning to "their end" in v. 17, which refers to death (in v. 17, the death of the wicked). Thus v. 24b has reference to what is to take place *after death,* not in this life. (2) The verb "receive" in Hebrew is the same word used to describe the taking up of Enoch (*Genesis* 5:24) and Elijah (*II Kings* 2:1; etc.) to be with God (it is the same word used in *Psalm* 49:15, which is discussed in Lesson X). (3) The wicked will be separated from their wealth and honor at death; but if death also severs the psalmist's relationship to God, he is not really any better off than they are. Indeed, his point seems to be that there is one thing which death cannot sever, and that is a godly man's communion with God. Thus, like *Psalm* 49:15, this verse indicates the Old Testament belief in life with God after death.

Psalm 92

This psalm was written by a man who had recently been attacked in some way by enemies (vss. 7, 9, 11). Since they were God's enemies (v. 9), they were also his enemies (v. 11). Like grass, they flourished for a while (v. 7), but God soon cut them off (vss. 7, 9, 11), and exalted the psalmist (v. 10). Apparently he is a priest or a temple singer, for he is familiar with the temple and its courts (v. 13), he is skilled at playing different kinds of instruments that were used to accompany psalms used in the temple worship (the lute or ten-stringed instrument, the harp, and the lyre, v. 3), and he is accustomed to singing praises to God for his wonderful works (vss. 1-4).

The thought of this psalm is so closely knit together that it seems to defy being subdivided into smaller units. The poet declares that he intends to praise God for his wonderful works (vss. 1-4), and then enumerates these as the overthrow of the wicked and the exaltation of the righteous (vss. 5-15). Apparently he deliberately distinguishes between the temporary "flourishing" of the wicked (v. 7), and the permanent "flourishing" of the righteous (vss. 12-13).

It is clear to the righteous from God's works (of overthrowing the wicked and exalting the righteous) that God is characterized by "steadfast love" and "faithfulness" (v. 2). But the "dull" or "stupid" man cannot see this because he looks only at present appearances (v. 7; see *Psalm* 73:22), and not at eternal results (v. 8). It was the psalmist's own experience that helped him see beyond the temporary to the permanent. When enemies threatened him, God exalted his strength ("horn") like that of the wild ox, and poured fresh oil over him (v. 10). The meaning of this last figure is difficult to determine. (a) It might suggest that God had recently had the author anointed king (see *I Samuel* 16:1, 13), and opposition by enemies did not and could not thwart God's deliberate act (see *Psalm* 2:1-9). (b) It might suggest that the psalmist had had leprosy, but when he was healed the priest poured oil on him to cleanse him ceremonially according to the law (see *Leviticus* 14:15-18). (c) It could mean that the poet. had been wounded or had a disease characterized by sores breaking out on his body, and the oil was used for healing purposes (see *Luke* 10:34). The allusions to his enemies in the surrounding verses (vss. 9, 11) would seem to support the idea that he had been wounded. (d) It might be a figurative expression meaning "joy" (see *Psalm* 45:7; *Isaiah* 61:3). This would fit with the first line in this verse, which uses "horn" as a symbol of strength.

The contrast between the "flourishing" of the wicked

and of the righteous is very striking. The wicked "flourish"—
the psalmist admits this (v. 7)—but only temporarily. They
are like "grass," which soon withers and is destroyed. But the
righteous "flourish" "like the palm tree" or "a cedar in
Lebanon" (v. 12) "in the courts of our God" (v. 13). The
point is that wickedness is not the way to a full life. It cannot
come from one's own resources, but only through constant
communion with God. Only when God is allowed to live in
one's heart can he be truly fruitful even in old age, and
genuinely strong ("full of sap") and beautiful ("green") (v.
14). And when other men see this kind of life, they see a
living demonstration that "the Lord is upright," for only
through his power can such a life be lived (v. 15).

Psalm 23

This song is the favorite of all the psalms throughout the
world. It was written by a man who had recently been
delivered from a severe illness from which he almost died (v.
4), and from enemies that sought to destroy him (v. 5). He is
keenly aware that he was not delivered by his own power or
by chance, but by God. He comes to the temple (v. 6) and
thanks God for intervening to save him from his troubles. He
does this by using two very common oriental figures: (1) the
shepherd (vss. 1-4); and (2) the host (vss. 5-6). It could be
that the poet is a king, because he refers to the Lord as his
"shepherd" (v. 1), and a king is frequently called the
shepherd of his people in ancient Near Eastern literature. In
Israel, the ideal king would willingly subject himself to the
rule of God. Futhermore, the reference to the Lord
"anointing" the psalmist (v. 5) might suggest that he is king.

In vss. 1-4, the poet uses the figure of the shepherd to
emphasize his appreciation for God's providing all his needs
(vss. 1-2), guiding him in safe paths (v. 3), and protecting him
from dangers (v. 4). That he is a servant of God does not
immune the psalmist from suffering and affliction. But
because God is "with him" (v. 4), he cannot be overcome,
and therefore he "fears no evil" ("evil" here means calamity,
as is often the case in the Bible, v. 4). God does not bless the
author's life because of his goodness or good works, but "for

his name's sake" (v. 3). He is "good" and "merciful" (v. 6; the Hebrew word translated "mercy" here in RSV means literally "steadfast love"), and he could not be otherwise and be true to his name (that is, his real nature). It is natural for him to love and care for and protect his people, because that is the kind of God he is. As frequently in the Bible, the word "soul" in v. 3 means the whole person. To "restore the soul" means to revive a person's spirits when he is down and out (see *Psalm* 19:7). God had done this by delivering the psalmist from his illness and his enemies.

In vss. 5-6, the poet pictures God as his host. The "house" where he has come for a meal at the host's invitation (v. 6) is the Jerusalem temple. The meal ("table") that is set before him (v. 5) is the sacrificial meal connected with the offering of thanksgiving that the worshipper brought to express his gratitude to God for what he had done for him (see *Leviticus* 7:11-17). It was a common courtesy to anoint the guest with oil (see *Luke* 7:36-50, especially v. 46), and to give him a full cup of wine with his meal (see *Genesis* 14:18; 27:25; *I Samuel* 16:20; 25:18; *II Samuel* 16:1-2) (v. 5). This demonstrated the genuineness of the host's hospitality and the generosity of his character. The psalmist is amazed at the limitless generosity of God's love and care in his own life, and he knows that it will continue "all the days of his life" (v. 6). The synonymous parallelism in v. 6 makes it clear that "for ever" in the second line means "all the days of his life" in the first.

REVIEW QUESTIONS

1. Give a two point outline of *Psalm* 73, then tell in your own words the content of this psalm.

2. What caused the author of *Psalm* 73 to doubt the goodness of God? Vss. 1-14. Have you ever had such doubts? Does it appear to you that wicked men are as blessed as or even more blessed than the righteous? Does it ever seem to you that living a God-centered life is vain? Discuss at length. Be very honest with yourself and the rest of the class in this discussion.

3. How did the author of *Psalm* 73 solve his problem of doubt? Vss. 15-28. Does his solution speak to your needs? Do you ever experience in a worshipping situation what this psalmist experienced at the temple? Discuss frankly your own feelings about the value of worship to the troubled heart.

4. Study carefully *Psalm* 73:24. Read several good commentaries on this passage. According to the author of this booklet, what does this verse mean? What arguments are given to support this view? What is your own position? What arguments do you have to support your view? Discuss at length.

5. Discuss the problems faced by the author of *Psalm* 92. Have you ever faced similar problems? Share your experiences with the class.

6. Study carefully and compare the statements having to do with pouring oil over the psalmists' heads in *Psalm* 92:10 and 23:5. Give your own view as to the meaning of the two expressions in these texts, and support it with good arguments in each case.

7. Contrast the "flourishing" of the wicked in *Psalm* 92:7 with the "flourishing" of the righteous in vss. 12-13. What practical lesson can the modern Christian learn from this? Discuss.

8. Describe the problems confronted by the author of *Psalm* 23. Have you ever faced similar problems? Share your experiences with the class.

9. What two figures does the author of *Psalm* 23 use to express the close relationship he feels with God? What does he emphasize in connection with each figure? What practical lessons do you receive from this? Discuss.

Lesson XII

GOD-CENTERED LIVING (II)

"Whom have I in heaven but thee?
And there is nothing upon earth
that I desire besides thee." (Psalm 73:25).

Psalm 1

This psalm forms a fitting introduction to the entire Psalter, as it summarizes in a brief, but powerful way the contrast between the fruitfulness of the righteous (vss. 1-3) and the insecurity of the wicked (vss. 4-6).

In vss. 1-3, the author describes the way a righteous man lives. First of all, speaking negatively, he resolutely refuses to follow the advice of the wicked, to follow the example of sinners, or to cast his lot with those who scoff at sincere devotion to God (v. 1). In no way is this to be taken to imply that he is not to associate with such people, because then he could hardly bear fruit for good in his life, as v. 3 affirms that he does. Instead, it means that as he associates with them, he is to maintain his commitment to God alone so as to be an influence on them, instead of allowing them to affect him for evil.

Secondly, speaking positively, the righteous man is wholly engulfed in studying and doing God's law (v. 2). He is not one who looks on God's teaching as a burden. On the contrary, he "delights in" the word of the Lord, and "meditates on" it all the time (see *Joshua* 1:8; *Matthew* 11:28-30; *I John* 5:2-3). It is his very life, and therefore he is wholly absorbed in its real message for him, and not in finding obscure rules for establishing some sort of legalistic system to bind on others (as the Pharisees did, *Matthew* 23:4).

Thirdly, speaking by way of illustration, the servant of God is like a tree, not just any tree located anywhere, but a tree that receives life from an inexhaustible source, continues to grow stronger and stronger and more and more beautiful, and naturally bears fruit to bless others (v. 3). The poet makes it clear that such a person is not empowered by his own strength, but is given his energy from God. He shows that he is never what he can become, but keeps growing toward the ideal. And he demonstrates that he does not have to be coerced to share what he has received, but does so naturally and freely.

In vss. 4-6, the psalmist depicts the insecurity of the wicked. There is nothing of substance in his life. He is of no use to others, but is like chaff (v. 4). Therefore, he cannot "stand" (endure) in the judgment (v. 5). Some scholars take "judgment" to mean the last judgment. However, the next line, which stands in synonymous parallelism to this line, says that sinners cannot stand in the congregation of the righteous. Thus, it seems more likely that he has in mind a judgment that God brings on the wicked in this life, probably a disfellowshipping or excommunication from the congregation of God's people, and consequently from the rich blessings that can be experienced only in this communion. This judgment is due to the wicked man's deliberate determination to live his life separate from God, and not to an arbitrary act of God. When the author says that God "knows" the way of the righteous, it is clear that he does not mean that God is "aware of" what the good man is doing (for the same thing is true of the wicked man). Rather, he means that God "has an intimate personal relationship with" the righteous man (see the word "know" in *Genesis* 4:1), and that he "has an active interest in" his manner of life (v. 6). Such a message as this is true only if God works actively in his world.

Psalm 127

Although a number of scholars believe that this poem is

composed of two originally independent sayings, the similarity of theme in the two parts of this psalm seems to argue in favor of its unity. Its fundamental truth is that the Lord is responsible for every human success or achievement, and man is wholly dependent on him in every phase of life. This does not mean that man is to be idle or lazy, but that he is to recognize his limitations and that he is to give God all the credit for anything he does.

The author gives four illustrations of this principle. (1) Such a common activity as building a house in which to live is doomed to failure unless God supports it (v. 1). Some have thought that the house here is the temple, but the common activities that follow suggests that it is a man's own dwelling. Others think it refers to the family, but since the family is treated in vss. 3-5, it is more likely that v. 1 intends a man's abode. The way in which God builds is not specified. The following illustrations would seem to allow several possibilities. Perhaps he means that God gives man the strength to build a house, the material to build it, and adequate time and skill to accomplish his task. Or possibly he means that man must not leave God out of any undertaking, no matter how insignificant it appears to him, because it will not survive without divine blessing.

(2) It is useless for a watchman to roam up and down the section of a city wall assigned to him, looking for signs of approaching danger from outside the wall, unless the Lord has determined that that city will not fall to the enemy (v. 1). (3) The farmer may work feverishly from dawn to dusk to clear his land and to plant his crop, but this is all futile unless the Lord gives life to the seed and causes them to produce a bumper crop. God gives more blessings to those he loves in a good night's sleep than they could ever acquire in endless days of anxious toil (v. 2).

(4) The bearing and raising of children are successful and profitable only through God's help (vss. 3-5). Children are God's gifts to parents (v. 3). If they are raised in the fear of God, they serve to protect the parents like arrows protect a soldier from the enemy (v. 4). In particular, the psalmist has

in mind charges or accusations brought against the father in a lawsuit. Court cases were ordinarily conducted just within the gate of the walled city (see *Ruth* 4:1). The man who enjoyed the support of his children would be in a much better position to resist or survive false charges than one who had to stand alone (v. 5).

Psalm 128

This psalm was composed in Jerusalem (v. 5). It was probably used by a priest or cult prophet to bless pilgrims that came from distant places to Jerusalem to worship at some festival. It seems to be a closely knit unit that defies subdivision.

The author describes seven blessings (vss. 1, 4, 5) that God bestows on those that "fear" him (vss. 1, 4). Synonymous parallelism in other texts show that "fearing" God in the wisdom and devotional literature of the Old Testament does *not* mean to "be afraid of" him, but to "stand in awe of" him (*Psalms* 33:8; 22:23), "reverence" him, "honor" him, "hold him in the highest respect or regard," etc. This is certainly the case here, but verse 1 shows that the specific emphasis that this poet has in mind is "walking in his ways," i.e., living a godly life.

According to this psalmist, the seven ways that God blesses the man who fears him are these: (1) He will not be deprived of the produce from his field or vineyard by a crop failure or exactions by tax collectors (v. 2); (2) He will live a happy life (v. 2); (3) He will enjoy good health (v. 2); (4) His wife will be healthy and bear him several children (v. 3); (5) His children will be healthy and well-adjusted in his home (v. 3); (6) He will find a thriving and prosperous city each time he comes to Jerusalem (v. 5); and (7) He will enjoy the blessing of grandchildren in his old age (v. 6). Such promises are not to be understood as invariable divine rules, but as generally the case. The fallacy of taking them as invariable rules is seen in such instances as Job's calamities or Jesus' crucifixion.

This psalm extols the importance of unity among brothers. But the text does not make clear precisely what the author had in mind originally. This has led to two major interpretations of this brief song. (1) Some scholars think that it has reference to blood brothers in the same family. When the father died, the traditional practice was for the sons to stay on the family inheritance and work the land together. But as the nation of Israel grew economically and the population moved to central localities and increased the size of cities, there was a great temptation for sons to move away from the family estate. If this is the background, the author of *Psalm* 133 is urging younger men in a family to remain on the ancestral property and farm it. (2) It seems more likely, however, that this poem is concerned with preserving unity among the people of God. Thus, it probably comes from a time when the spirit of friction and division was rampant in the land. This could have been any number of things, as strife between Israel and Judah, or struggles between rich and poor in Israel or Judah or both, or conflicts between political parties in Israel of Judah or both in which the warring factions were seeking to get their own champion on the throne, or the like.

The poet gives four reasons why God's people should be united. (1) It is good (v. 1). It is interesting that he gives no explanation as to why unity is good. Perhaps he does not need to do so, because this should be self-evident to everyone. Unity is good because brothers do things for each other (see *Philippians* 2:3-4), but there may be many other reasons as well. (2) It is pleasant (v. 1). Again the poet gives no reason for this. But it seems obvious that it is true because brothers do things together, not separately. Again, there may be other reasons as well. (3) It is fragrant and life-giving (vss. 2-3). The author vividly illustrates this with two similes. It is like precious oil that runs down on the high priest's beard, giving off a sweet-smelling fragrance (see *Exodus* 29:7; 30:22-33). It is also like the dew of Hermon that falls on the mountains of Zion. Many scholars point out that this is geographically impossible, and want to emend the Hebrew text to read "parched ground," "arid highlands," or "Ijon" (on the latter, see *I Kings* 15:20). However, it could be that the dew which appeared on Mount Hermon in such abundance each morning and was partly responsible for the luxuriant foliage on the landscape came to be proverbial, and is used here to denote the natural blessings that God showered on Jerusalem. Both of these illustrations emphasize the attractiveness of unity among God's people to those who observe, and the influence that this unity has on others to worship the God of a people that love each other so much (see *John* 17:20-21). (4) God blesses those who dwell together in unity, and that blessing is life for evermore (v. 3). The context seems to indicate that this does not refer to individual immortality after death (although this thought does occur in the Old Testament, as in *Psalms* 49:15 and 73:24), but to the continued life of the people of God as a vigorous body of God's servants.

Unfortunately, there is not enough information to allow one to be dogmatic as to whether this psalm originated in North Israel or in Judah. The reference to Mount Hermon in v. 3 might be used to favor North Israel, but the allusion to the mountains of Zion in the same verse points to Judah.

REVIEW QUESTIONS

1. Give a two point outline of *Psalm* 1, then tell in your own words the content of this psalm.

2. How does the author of *Psalm* 1 describe the righteous man in verses 1-2? Discuss each point and apply it to your own life.

3. What figure does the psalmist use in *Psalm* 1:3 to describe the righteous man? What figure does he use in verse 4 to describe the wicked man? Discuss each of these ideas at length.

4. What are the possible meanings of the word "judgment" in *Psalm* 1:5? Read a number of commentaries on this. Which do you think is the correct meaning? Support your view with good arguments.

5. List the four illustrations used by the author of *Psalm* 127 to show that the Lord is responsible for every human achievement. Discuss the practical significance of this truth in detail.

6. The author of *Psalm* 128 gives seven blessings that God bestows on the person who fears him. Name these and discuss the significance of this thought in human life.

7. What are two possible interpretations of *Psalm* 133? Which do you think is correct? Why?

8. Give the four reasons suggested by the author of *Psalm* 133 why God's people should be united. Discuss the meaning and significance of each of these.

9. What two illustrations are given in *Psalm* 133:2-3 to emphasize that unity is fragrant and life-giving? Discuss the importance of this in daily Christian living.

Lesson XIII

THE ESSENCE OF TRUE RELIGION

"For the love of Christ controls us, because we are convinced that one has died for all; therefore all have died. And he died for all, that those who live might live no longer for themselves but for him who for their sake died and was raised." (II Corinthians 5:14-15).

Not all religion is true religion. Some think true religion is to be equated with a meticulous obedience of certain external acts commanded in the Bible and interpreted in a specific way. While it is true that the man who loves God will do what he commands, many scriptures make it very clear that men can do these things and be far from practicing true religion; as a matter of fact, it is possible for man to do external acts that God commands and possess a religion contrary to what God desires (see *I Samuel* 15:22-23; *Isaiah* 1:10-17; 29:13-14; *Micah 6:6-8; Hosea 6:4-6;* Amos *5:21-24; Jeremiah* 7:21-29). The fundamental issue in all religion is its focal point or center of reference. An emphasis on obedience to external commands frequently leads to pride and self-exaltation. Human talent and achievement are at the center. This lesson calls attention to two psalms that emphasize true religion—a religion that has God at the center, and is built on trust in his grace and boasting in what he has done for sinners.

Psalm 40 (Psalm 70)

Many scholars· think that *Psalm* 40 was originally two independent psalms (vss. 1-11 and 12-17), which were later combined into one psalm. Two arguments are usually given in support of this view. (1) In vss. 1-11, the psalmist's problem is illness which has already been overcome, and thus he thanks God for delivering him; but in vss. 12-17, the poet's problem is persecution by enemies which has not been overcome, and thus he begs God to deliver him. (2) Vss. 13-17 are almost exactly identical with *Psalm* 70, which indicates that at one time this song circulated independently. Now while the facts used to support this view are correct, they can be interpreted in a different way. First, many of the psalms were written by individuals who were sick and who were being ridiculed or afflicted by enemies, and thus it is not unnatural to find these two themes combined in one psalm. Second, in several psalms the author refers back to past trials and deliverances as an encouragement that God would deliver him under present conditions. Perhaps this is the situation in *Psalm* 40. Third, it would be natural for one who went to the temple regularly to use one of the songs he had learned and grown to love there when he was faced with misfortune in his own life. This would explain this poet's use of a song which is also recorded in the Old Testament as *Psalm* 70.

The author of *Psalm* 40 was a "poor and needy" individual (v. 17) who had been stricken with a terrible disease and had almost died (v. 2). This was God's way of punishing him for his many sins (v. 12). His enemies took advantage of his helpless condition, sought opportunities to kill him, and longed for him to die from his disease (vss. 14-15). Instead of seeking help from "false gods" and their worshippers, he put his trust in God (v. 4). God delivered him before (v. 5), and he begs him to do so again (v. 11) in order that he might be able to tell "the great congregation" (vss. 9-10) what God had done for him (vss. 16-17), as he had done when God delivered him before (vss. 5, 9-10). This psalm seems to fall naturally into two parts. (1) The psalmist describes his earlier affliction, tells how God delivered him, and recalls how he proclaimed to his fellow worshippers how God had worked in his life (vss. 1-10). (2) He pleads with God to forgive him of his many sins which have brought new distresses upon him, and to spare him from the evils that his enemies are planning against him (vss. 11-17).

In vss. 1-10, the author describes his former experience.

He had become very sick and had almost died (this is what is meant by his descent into the "desolate pit" and the "miry bog" in v. 2; both of these terms are symbols for Sheol or the grave). But he prayed fervently and patiently to God, and God delivered him (v. 1). He pulled him out of the gaping jaws of death, and set him on a firm footing (v. 2). In this way, he put a "new song" in the poet's heart. In other words, when God delivered him, he yearned to tell others what God had done for him so that they too would put their trust in God (v. 3). The content of this "new song" is given in vss. 4-5. It is the man who trusts in the Lord (not in idols or their worshippers) that is blessed (v. 4). God has done so many good things for his people (note "us" in v. 5, which corresponds to "many" in v. 3) that it is impossible to number them (v. 5).

In gratitude to the Lord for what he did for his people, it was customary to bring sacrifices to him. But this psalmist knows that it is all too easy to make an outward show of religion, to give God his things or his possessions. He realizes that true religion demands that a person give God his whole being, and thus he says, "Lo, *I* come . . . *I* delight to do thy will, O God" (vss. 6-7). This does not mean that the Lord did not want sacrifices in Old Testament times, but rather that he accepted sacrifices only from those who first gave themselves to the Lord and loved God's teaching or law from the heart (v. 7). The inspired writers and speakers in Old Testament times knew quite well that "it is impossible that the blood of bulls and goats should take away sins" (*Hebrews* 10:3). But there were many Israelites who were satisfied with a diluted religion which they reduced to a certain number of rites and acts, and the same was true among Jewish Christians whom the author of Hebrews had in mind when he wrote *Hebrews* 10:3-4.

In light of God's great deliverance of the poet from severe illness, he enthusiastically declared to others what the Lord had done for him. His words are very striking: "I proclaim and tell" (v. 5); "I have told"; "I have not restrained my lips" (v. 9); " I have not hid thy saving help"; "I have spoken"; "I have not concealed thy steadfast love" (v. 10).

The thought is that it is both unnatural and sinful to refrain from telling others what God has done for the individual.

In vss. 11-17, the author begs God to deliver him from a present distress. He has sinned greatly, consequently "evils" or calamities have come upon him (v. 12), and thus he pleads for God's "mercy," "steadfast love," and "faithfulness" (v. 11). Such a plea, of course, assumes that God forgave men in Old Testament times. The psalmist's enemies rejoice at his calamities (v. 15), "seek to snatch away his life," and "desire his hurt" (v. 14). Thus, he pleads with God to put them to shame (vss. 14-15), and to cause those who seek him and love his salvation to rejoice (v. 16) by delivering him from his distresses (vss. 13, 17).

The speaker in *Psalm* 40 can hardly be Jesus Christ, because he is a sinner (v. 12) who needs God's mercy (v. 11). And yet, *Hebrews* 10:5-9 quotes *Psalm* 40:6-8 and puts these words into Christ's mouth. Apparently, the New Testament writer is using the Old Testament typologically here, and is selecting just those lines from *Psalm* 40 which are relevant to his point, without intending to imply that the whole psalm had Christ in mind.

Psalm 50

This psalm was composed in Jerusalem ("Zion," v. 2) after the temple was built and sacrifices were being offered on a regular basis (vss. 8-9). It comes from a time when the Jews strongly believed that what God really wanted was animal sacrifices offered at prescribed times and in prescribed ways. They also believed that their attitude toward and treatment of their fellowman had no relationship with religion (vss. 18-20), and concluded that God's failure to intervene and punish them for such practices (God's "silence," vss. 3, 21) was proof that he accepted their sacrifices as substitutes for daily godly living.

Psalm 50 seems to fall naturally into three parts. (1) The psalmist announces that God can no longer be silent, and that he comes to judge his people who trust in sacrifice (vss. 1-6).

(2) God comes and declares that his people cannot bribe him with their sacrifices (vss. 7-15). (3) God condemns the hypocrisy of those who profess to be loyal to the Lord, but who live ungodly lives (vss. 16-23).

In vss. 1-6, the poet describes in typical language the coming of the Lord to judge his people (see *Deuteronomy* 33:2; *Judges* 5:4-5; *Amos* 1:2; *Micah* 6:1-2). He "shines forth" out of Zion (v. 2). A devouring fire precedes him, and he is surrounded by a tempest (v. 3). He calls the heavens (vss. 4, 6) and the earth (vss. 1, 4) to be his witnesses as he presents his lawsuit or court case against his people, with whom he had entered into covenant at Sinai (v. 5). All the people who were present when God made his covenant with Israel at Sinai had died, but the heavens and the earth were there, and so God could appeal to them to support the truthfulness of his position. The covenant was sealed by sacrifice (v. 5), it is true, but sacrifices were not the central focus of the covenant. That was an intimate personal relationship with God from the heart. Thus, God comes to "judge" his people (v. 6), to make a distinction between those who were really faithful to the covenant and those who only professed to be.

In vss. 7-15, God begins by emphasizing that the major aspect of the covenant relationship is that the Lord took Israel unto himself to be his very own. He calls them "*my* people," and declares, "I am God, *your* God" (v. 7). In other words, the first and most fundamental aspect of the covenant was God's personal involvement in the lives of his people. Sacrifice was the natural expression of the people's love for God, who had delivered them out of Egypt and guided them in the wilderness (see *Exodus* 20:1-3). God did not condemn them for offering sacrifices (v. 8). Rather, he rebuked them for their misunderstanding of the nature of sacrifice, and for the goals that they sought to accomplish in offering sacrifices. They felt that when they offered God an animal sacrifice, they were obligating him to bless their lives because they were denying themselves to give him something. Thus, God declares clearly that they could not give him anything because it was already his, and the only reason they had it was that he gave it to them. He proclaims:

"Every beast of the forest *is mine*" (v. 10)
"All that moves in the field *is mine*" (v. 11)
"The world and all that is in it *is mine*" (v. 12).

When man does anything to manipulate God or to control God, he makes man the center of religion rather than God. That which binds the worshipper to God is central to genuine religion, but that which seeks to bind God to the worshipper is idolatry.

Pagan worshippers believed that their gods ate the blood and meat of their sacrifices, and thus they kept their gods alive by continually offering sacrifices for them. But the true God is completely independent of all things; as a matter of fact, they are all dependent on him. Thus God says:

"If I were hungry, I would not tell you" (v. 12).
"Do I eat the flesh of bulls,
 or drink the blood of goats?" (v. 13).

What God really wants of man is humble, grateful recognition that he is totally dependent on him, which is expressed most graphically when man turns to God for help in times of severest distress. Man glorifies God by calling on him in times of trouble (vss. 14-15).

In vss. 16-23, God speaks to the man who professes that he loves God, but who lives an ungodly life. He is "the wicked man" (v. 16). He is quite adept at quoting ("reciting") God's statutes and talking about God's covenant (v. 16), but he demonstrates his inner hatred of God's word by violating his precepts. He practices and associates with those who practice stealing, adultery (v. 18), and slander (vss. 19-20). And they feel very confident that they are safe, because they have been doing these things for some time and God had done nothing to stop them. But now God announces that he will be silent no longer, but will punish his hypocritical people who refuse to repent (v. 21). The psalm ends with God appealing to his people to repent lest they be destroyed, and to show genuine gratitude to God for what he has done for them in order that he might deliver them from this impending calamity (vss. 22-23). Sacrifice, indeed, had its place as an expression of the worshipper's appreciation for what God had done for him, but one could abuse this action by using it as a means of coercing or persuading God to intervene in behalf of a hypocritical pretender.

REVIEW QUESTIONS

1. Read carefully *Hosea* 6:4-6 and *Micah* 6:6-8. What two fundamental types of religion exist in the world today? Discuss each type carefully. Which do you think is correct? Why?

2. Give three arguments to show that *Psalm* 40 is a unit rather than two originally independent psalms that were later combined.

3. Describe the problems facing the author of *Psalm* 40. Have you ever had similar problems? Share your experiences with the class.

4. Give a two point outline of *Psalm* 40, then tell in your own words the content of this psalm.

5. Read carefully *Psalm* 40:6-7. Discuss the nature of true religion as it is described here. Does the New Testament teach virtually the same thing in *Hebrews* 10:3-4? Discuss the meaning of these verses. Tell how the author of Hebrews applies *Psalm* 40:6-8 in *Hebrews* 10:5-9.

6. Study carefully *Psalm* 40:5, 9-10. What lesson can we learn from this concerning the responsiblity of one who has been blessed or delivered by God? Is this practical in your own life? Discuss.

7. Give a three point outline of *Psalm* 50, then tell in you own words the content of this psalm.

8. Describe the Lord's coming as it is presented in *Psalm* 50:1-6. What is meant by all this? Use commentaries in your private research.

9. According to *Psalm* 50:7, what is the primary aspect of the covenant relationship between God and his people? How does sacrifice (or any external act of religion) function in this type of relationship? Verses 8-13. What does God really want from his worshippers? Verses 14-15.

10. Read carefully *Psalm* 50:16-20. Define and describe the hypocrisy of God's people as it is depicted in this passage. Do you feel we have this problem in the church today? Discuss in detail.

BIBLIOGRAPHY

Since these three volumes on the Old Testament Psalms are designed for the non-specialist in the field, it has been deemed best to avoid referring to or quoting from scholarly works except in a few cases where it was absolutely necessary. Studies on the Psalms are "legion" even in English, to say nothing of monographs, commentaries, special treatments, etc., in other languages. Here are suggested only a very few works which may offer further aid to the student who desires to probe more deeply into the Psalms.

Introductions and Commentaries

Anderson, G. W. "The Psalms," *Peake's Commentary on the Bible*. London: Thomas Nelson and Sons Ltd., Reprinted 1967.

Barnes, W. E. "The Psalms," *The Westminster Commentary on the Bible*. London: Methuen and Co., Ltd., 1931.

Barth, C. *Introduction to the Psalms.* New York: Charles Scribner's Sons, 1966.

Briggs, C. A. and E. G. *The International Critical Commentary*. New York: Charles Scribner's Sons, 1906. 2 volumes.

Buttenwieser, M. *The Psalms Chronologically Treated*. Chicago: The University of Chicago Press, 1938.

Dahood, M. *Psalms. The Anchor Bible*. Garden City, N.Y.: Doubleday & Co., 1966-1970. 3 volumes.

Eaton, J. H. *Psalms. The Torch Bible Commentaries*. London: SCM Press, 1964.

Fohrer, G. "The Psalter," *Introduction to the Old Testament*. Nashville: Abingdon Press, 1965, pp. 280-295.

Kissane, E. J. *The Book of Psalms*. Dublin: Browne and Nolan, Ltd. 1964.

Leslie, E. A. *The Psalms*. Nashville: Abingdon Press, 1949.

McCullough, W. S., and others, *The Interpreter's Bible*, Vol. IV. Nashville: Abingdon Press, 1955.

Murphy, R. E. "Psalms," *The Jerome Biblical Commentary*. Englewood Cliffs, N. J.: Prentice-Hall Inc., 1968.

Toombs, L. E. "The Psalms," *The Interpreter's One-Volume Commentary on the Bible*. Nashville: Abingdon Press, 1971.

Weiser, A. *Psalms. The Old Testament Library*. Philadelphia: The Westminster Press, 1969.

Special Studies on Various Aspects of Psalm Studies

Blenkinsopp, J. "Can We Pray the Cursing Psalms?" *Clergy Review*, Vol. 50 (1965), pp. 534-538.

de Boer, P. A. H. *Studies on Psalms. Oudtestamentische Studien*. Vol. XIII. Leiden: E. J. Brill, 1963.

Crim, K. R. *The Royal Psalms*. Richmond: John Knox Press, 1962.

Engnell, I. *A Rigid Scrutiny*. Nashville: Vanderbilt University Press, 1969.

Hempel, J. "Psalms, Book of," *The Interpreter's Dictionary of the Bible*. Vol. III. Nashville: Abingdon Press, 1962, pp. 942-958.

James, F. *Thirty Psalmists*. New York: Seabury, 1965.

McKeating, H. "Divine Forgiveness in the Psalms," *Scottish Journal of Theology*, Vol. 18 (1965), pp. 69-83.

Mowinckel, S. *The Psalms in Israel's Worship*. Oxford: At the university Press, 1963. 2 volumes.

Peters, J. P. *The Psalms as Liturgies*. New York: The Macmillan Co., 1922.

Ringgren, H. *The Faith of the Psalmists*. London: SCM Press, 1963.

Snaith, N. "Selah," *Vetus Testamentum,* Vol. 2 (1952), pp. 43-56.

Terrien, S. *The Psalms and their Meaning for Today*. 1952.

Westermann, C. *The Praise of God in the Psalms*. Richmond: John Knox Press, 1965.

INDEX

Psalm	Volume and Lesson	Psalm	Volume and Lesson
130	II, IX	137	III, I
132	I, XII	139	III, VII
133	III, XII	147	I, XIII
135	I, XI	148	I, VIII
136	I, XI	150	I, VI